des affaires

POUR

LES NULS

L'anglais des affaires POUR LES NULS

Claude Raimond

FIRST Editions

L'anglais des affaires pour les Nuls

ISBN : 978-2-7540-1519-6
Dépôt légal : 4e trimestre 2009

Imprimé en France par Hérissey à Évreux (Eure) - N° 116847

Édition : Véronique Marta
Correction : Jacqueline Rouzet
Mise en page : KN Conception
Production : Emmanuelle Clément

Éditions First-Gründ
60, rue Mazarine
75006 Paris – France
Tél. : 01 45 49 60 00
Fax : 01 45 49 60 01
Internet : www.editionsfirst.fr
www.pourlesnuls.fr

Sommaire

Introduction

Bienvenue dans *L'anglais des affaires pour les Nuls*, l'anglais de la vie professionnelle, pour lecteurs francophones aux prises avec l'anglais.

Est-ce à dire que cette langue nous oppose des obstacles que ne rencontrent pas les autres ? Serait-elle plus difficile pour nous, alors qu'elle comporte tant de mots proches du français ?

Eh bien oui ! L'anglais est difficile pour tous, et il comporte des difficultés supplémentaires pour les personnes de langue maternelle française. Mais avant d'examiner ces difficultés et la manière de les surmonter, il importe de dissiper un malentendu.

Le mythe de l'anglais facile

L'anglais paraît facile aux résidents d'Europe continentale parce qu'ils peuvent aisément acquérir assez d'anglais pour communiquer tant bien que mal entre eux. Leurs langues offrent avec l'anglais des analogies résultant de sources communes comme le latin et les parlers germaniques. Et comme les langues d'Europe ont beaucoup emprunté les unes aux autres, elles foisonnent de mots qui se ressemblent. Ces ressemblances sont autant de passerelles vers un premier niveau d'anglais que certains appellent *globish*, contraction de *global English*, et que d'autres, peut-être parce que *globish* rime avec *rubbish*, préfèrent appeler *international English*.

Malheureusement, il n'y a pas de passerelle et encore moins d'ascenseur vers l'étage supérieur des anglophones natifs. Pour s'en approcher, il faut gravir la pente et surmonter une à une les difficultés de leur langue :

- ampleur du vocabulaire
- nombreux homonymes
- nombreux homophones, ces mots de prononciation identique mais d'orthographe et de sens différents
- foisonnement d'expressions idiomatiques
- le sens de nombreux mots change de manière subtile ou radicale selon le contexte
- la prononciation n'est pas une mince affaire
  - plus de phonèmes – plus de sons différents – que dans presque toutes les autres langues
  - un même son peut s'écrire de trois à cinq manières différentes, et une même combinaison de lettres produire de trois à cinq sons différents
  - la prononciation change d'un pays à un autre
- les différents pays anglophones n'utilisent pas tous les mêmes expressions idiomatiques ni la même orthographe, et ne désignent pas de la même manière divers objets ou fonctions de la vie courante.

Allez-vous baisser les bras, renoncer à communiquer avec le monde anglophone ? Si vous ne pouvez pas vous offrir ce luxe, la seule option disponible est alors de retrousser vos manches et de prendre le taureau par les cornes. Rassurez-vous, ce livre vous aide à surmonter les difficultés de l'anglais, et en prime, il vous indique des passerelles du français vers l'anglais, en vous précisant où poser les pieds quand leur usage comporte des risques. En voici une à emprunter en toute sécurité : *the only option available then is to roll up your sleeves and to take the bull by the horns*, avec deux images rendues exactement de la même façon dans les deux langues.

Conforté par ces promesses, vous désirez maintenant des précisions sur les handicaps des francophones.

Les handicaps des francophones

Pas doués pour les langues ?

Toute langue entendue par un enfant lorsqu'il apprend à parler influe sur ses aptitudes linguistiques. S'il n'en entend qu'une, elle peut entraîner des handicaps difficiles à surmonter.

Les Asiatiques distinguent mal les sons 'l' et 'r', et pour les Hispaniques, le 'b' et le 'v' sont difficiles à départager. Leur mauvaise prononciation de ces consonnes est reconnue comme un accent étranger, mais ne nuit pas outre mesure à la compréhension lorsqu'ils parlent ou entendent une autre langue.

Les particularités du français sont plus lourdes de conséquences. Le français est la seule langue d'Europe dans laquelle la position de l'accent tonique et la durée des sons de voyelle ne servent pas à reconnaître les mots. Dans les autres langues, ces deux éléments établissent entre les mots des distinctions apportant du sens. Ils sont marqués par les locuteurs et sont remarqués par eux. Un francophone pur et dur n'entend pas d'accent tonique et n'a pas conscience de la durée des sons dans sa langue, ce qui ne servirait à rien, mais pas non plus dans les autres, ce qui l'empêche souvent de comprendre ou d'être compris. L'affirmation « les Français ne sont pas doués pour les langues » est en partie justifiée par cette incapacité découlant de propriétés du français. Les effets en sont encore plus néfastes à l'égard de l'anglais, car ils se combinent à ses autres difficultés.

Le problème des différences

L'anglais nous rappelant le français, sa pratique active de manière intempestive des éléments du répertoire de phrases et de sons français accumulés dans notre subconscient. L'influence du français peut nous aider à comprendre ou à nous exprimer, mais elle est plus souvent pernicieuse. Elle est responsable de la quasi-totalité de nos incompréhensions ou erreurs lors des tests ou examens d'anglais ou dans nos contacts avec des anglophones.

Cette influence peut être atténuée en multipliant les contacts avec l'anglais ou en l'apprenant par immersion. Elle peut être déjouée par une approche préventive, en signalant pour toute phrase anglaise les points où l'influence du français risque de provoquer la mauvaise prononciation, le malentendu, la faute d'anglais. C'est l'approche utilisée dans ce livre.

À qui s'adresse ce livre

Plusieurs hypothèses relatives à votre rapport aux langues, vos besoins et vos préférences m'ont guidé dans la préparation de l'ouvrage :

- Vous parvenez à vous débrouiller en anglais avec des Allemands, des Italiens ou des Chinois, mais vous ne comprenez pas tout ce que vous lisez et vous comprenez encore moins ce que disent les anglophones.
- L'interprétation simultanée ne fait pas encore partie des services dont vous disposez pour vous rendre à l'étranger ou téléphoner à des personnages importants.
- Vous savez que la plupart des employeurs exigent désormais un niveau d'anglais certifié par des tests comme le TOEIC (Test Of English for International Communication), et vous cherchez un emploi ou aimeriez en changer.

- Vous souhaitez progresser rapidement mais sûrement, en consolidant à chaque pas votre acquis antérieur.
- Vous ne pensez pas qu'il faille souffrir pour apprendre une langue et vous ne voulez pas vous soumettre à des exercices fastidieux.

Si vous vous reconnaissez dans cette liste, ce livre est fait pour vous.

Organisation du livre

Le livre répartit le vocabulaire professionnel et ses modalités d'utilisation sur trois parties divisées en chapitres. Ces chapitres sont écrits en anglais avec des aménagements vous permettant de les comprendre.

En annexe, un lexique français/anglais reprend tout le vocabulaire anglais du livre.

Trois parties allant du général au particulier

La première partie, *Le travail en général*, traite de sujets communs à la plupart des activités : recherche d'emploi ; trajets pour se rendre au travail ; réunions internes ; retraite. Dans la deuxième partie, *À l'intérieur d'une organisation*, vous verrez tourner certains rouages de tout organisme professionnel : le téléphone ; les rapports, mémos et courriers électroniques ; la comptabilité. La troisième et dernière partie, *Échanges et commerce*, est consacrée aux échanges et aux activités qui les sous-tendent : les présentations commerciales ; les négociations ; la distribution ; les banques de détail.

Organisation des chapitres

Chaque chapitre est organisé selon un modèle unique conçu pour relever les défis de l'anglais : ampleur du vocabulaire, aléas de la prononciation, expressions idiomatiques, et pour nous autres francophones, surdité à l'opposition sons brefs/long et au placement de l'accent tonique, dérapages sous l'influence du français.

Un chapitre est divisé en trois sections : textes, commentaires, lexique français/anglais.

Certains mots ou expressions apparaissant pour la première fois dans le chapitre sont en **gras**. Leur équivalent français figure dans la section *Vocabulaire Anglais/Français*.

Vous verrez aussi, insérés de loin en loin dans les textes et commentaires (*entre parenthèses et en italique*), des équivalents anglais pour comprendre sans traduire. Vous connaîtrez déjà certains de ces synonymes, et vous en comprendrez d'autres, proches du français. Exemple : 'John, as head (*chief*) of the regional office, chairs (*presides over*) the meeting.'

Ce procédé tire parti de la surabondance du vocabulaire anglais tout en vous aidant à la maîtriser.

Des textes anglais centrés sur un même thème

La première section entre dans le vif du sujet avec de l'anglais directement utilisable dans votre vie professionnelle : discussion, exposé, lettre, courrier électronique ou autre document. D'autres textes apportent des précisions ou des éclairages pour vous aider à formuler en anglais vos propres choix ou orientations.

Commentaires

Ces commentaires portent sur des mots ou groupes de mots figurant dans les textes. Quatre sous-sections portent chacune sur une classe de commentaires : prononciation, confusions possibles, associations de mots fréquentes, ressemblances utiles avec le français. Les fragments de texte sont reproduits et commentés dans l'ordre d'apparition à l'intérieur des textes.

Un commentaire ne se limite pas à un élément du fragment reproduit. Il donne d'autres exemples qui vous aident à assimiler les règles, exceptions ou mises en gardes présentées tout en étendant votre vocabulaire.

Des infos sur la prononciation et l'accentuation

La première classe de commentaires, *Prononcez correctement !* utilise des extraits des textes pour illustrer des schémas récurrents de prononciation ou d'accentuation ou des exceptions à ces schémas.

Les mots qui ressemblent à d'autres pour qui ne perçoit pas la durée des syllabes sont opposés à ceux avec lesquels ils peuvent être confondus : *paper/ pepper, bin/been, sheep/ship, cost/coast...*

Pour indiquer la prononciation, cette sous-section établit des analogies avec des mots courants. Exemple : le ow du Dow Jones index est prononcé comme le ow de *cow* ou le *ao* de *ciao*, non comme le *oa* de *road* ou le *o* de *spoke*.

Les différences

Cette classe de commentaires est intitulée *Un homme averti en vaut deux*. Elle vous met en garde contre des erreurs résultant de la méconnaissance de certaines différences.

Dans le cas de différence entre l'anglais et le français, le but est d'éviter l'influence du français, par exemple l'emploi du *present perfect* au lieu du *simple past*, là où nous utiliserions le passé composé, proche du *present perfect*. Ainsi dans la phrase : *I saw an outstanding film yesterday* (J'ai vu hier un film excellent), nous devons nous retenir de dire ou d'écrire *I have seen…*, comme le suggère notre réflexe francophone.

Les commentaires peuvent souligner des différences entre des expressions anglaises que nous risquons de confondre, comme *row* (rangée) qui rime avec *slow*, et *row* (dispute) qui rime avec *cow*, ou des différences d'usage entre l'anglais des Américains et celui des Britanniques, comme *car park* (au Royaume-Uni) au lieu de *parking lot* aux états-Unis.

L'effet préventif du commentaire est renforcé en citant d'autres cas du type d'erreur ou de confusion signalé. Exemple : le français termine par un 'e' de nombreux mots dont les homologues anglais ne comportent pas cette lettre. Un commentaire le rappelant à propos de synonym pourrait citer *paradox, act, autodidact, paragraph, enthusiasm, sarcasm, herb.*

À RETENIR

Des mots qui vont très bien ensemble

Ce titre évocateur annonce des associations de mots figurant dans les textes du chapitre, et que vous rencontrerez à coup sûr en pratiquant l'anglais. Si vous les mémorisez, la rencontre d'un de leurs éléments vous rappellera l'autre ou les autres, accélérant votre compréhension et votre production.

Par exemple, il est fréquent d'associer au mot career l'un des adjectifs *successful, brilliant, exciting, long,* ou *uneventful, boring.* Ayant entendu le début de phrase *After a long and successful…*, vous attendez le mot *career.*

Une association de mots présentée dans cette classe de commentaires est complétée par d'autres associations d'un ou plusieurs de ces mots.

Des passerelles

Après avoir vu les difficultés que présente l'anglais, voici un peu de réconfort ! Ce chapitre vous montre des formes ou des mots proches du français que nous comprenons aussitôt et pouvons utiliser sans risque.

Lexique anglais/français

La troisième section donne une traduction française des mots ou expressions en **gras** dans les textes ou commentaires. Un même terme peut figurer dans un autre chapitre et dans son lexique avec un sens différent.

Et maintenant...

Informé en détail sur le contenu du livre, vous pouvez l'utiliser à votre guise. Un chapitre comble d'éventuelles lacunes lexicales ou grammaticales, consolide et développe vos connaissances, mais sa lecture ne conditionne pas la compréhension des autres. La seule raison qui pourrait vous inciter à tout lire d'un bout à l'autre, c'est qu'ainsi vous seriez sûr de n'avoir rien oublié.

Vous pouvez commencer par le chapitre correspondant le mieux à vos soucis du moment et même le lire dans l'ordre qui vous convient. *And now, go for it!*

Première partie

Le travail en général

Cette partie vous permet de vivre et d'évoquer en anglais des moments classiques de toute vie professionnelle. Le chapitre 1 porte sur **la recherche d'emploi**. Le chapitre 2 est consacré au **trajet**, transition entre travail et vie personnelle. Le 3e chapitre, **Réunions internes**, décrit les inévitables réunions. Le quatrième et dernier chapitre, **La retraite**, examine différents aspects de l'aboutissement normal d'une vie professionnelle.

Chapitre 1

La recherche d'emploi

Dans ce chapitre

- L'importance du CV
- La lettre de motivation
- Pensez à Internet
- L'entrevue

Un mail encourageant

After sending dozens of letters in response to job **ads** in the **trade press**, you received a number of replies, some bluntly rejecting your **application**, others **extolling** your **credentials** (*qualifications*) but mentioning with regret that a candidate more suitable has been selected and wishing you good luck with your job search. You were beginning to despair when the following e-mail finally arrived.

***

From: Caroline Weatherspoon <carolinew@rubberfoam.com>

Date: July 10, 2009

To: Robert Bourgeois <bobbourgeois@gmail.com>

Subject: Your application

Mr Bourgeois,

Thank you for responding to (*for answering*) our recruiting ad. Your professional experience as well as your educational background are impressive and seem to correspond to our requirements (*exigencies*) for the position. We have retained your application for further consideration and I would like to discuss it with you.

We are inviting several **applicants** (*candidates*) to **meet with** me and possibly with John Riverside, head of our manufacturing department within which the person **eventually hired** will manage quality assurance. We would like to reach (*come to, arrive at*) a final decision by the end of this month. Could you come to my office for an interview next Wednesday, July 15 at 10 a.m.? Should this date and time be inconvenient, please call Nancy Woods on 881 809 331 to make other arrangements.

We are looking forward to **meeting** you (*making your acquaintance*) very soon (*shortly, in the coming days*).

Best regards,

Caroline Weatherspoon, Manager, Human Resources.

***

This e-mail is your reward for having prepared and used your application documents according to sensible ideas such as those presented in the two following texts. But you've only won the first battle. To win the war – to get a job offer – you must shine (*be brilliant*) during the interview, the challenges of which are described in the last text of the chapter.

Questions à considérer avant de préparer et d'envoyer un CV

Many people are ill at ease (*uncomfortable, embarrassed*) when **looking for** a job, thinking they lack (*don't have*) what it takes (*what is **required***) to sell themselves. Yet (*however*) being asked to an interview is similar to enticing a **potential customer** to enter a shop, and obtaining a job offer is **akin to** (*of a similar nature as*) **completing** (*closing*) a sale.

Looking at the problem from the buyer's perspective (*viewpoint*) raises following questions:

1 What kind of talent are they really looking for (*trying to find*) and why?

2 What might cause them to reject your application?

3 What elements in your profile might they regard as pluses?

4 What elements in your profile might they regard as minuses?

5 How many application letters are they likely to receive?

6 How many candidates will they likely interview?

If you are sending off your CV to an organisation advertising a **job vacancy**, the ad itself will answer the first question, but only a tiny (*minuscule*) fraction of questions 2, 3 and 4. To answer them, you need much more information than that provided by the recruiting ad. You want to know what type of organisation it is; if a company, whether it is privately owned or public, in the latter case, who the **shareholders** (***stockholders***) are; how many people it employs in your region and elsewhere; how the organisation has evolved since its **inception** (*beginning*) and how it is likely to evolve in the future.

Twenty years ago, getting answers to all above questions would have been a **daunting** (*an intimidating*) task. Today, you can get at least **tentative** (*preliminary*) answers to most of them in half an hour to an hour of Internet surfing. Once your résumé has been **tweaked** (*adjusted*) in the right direction, you can then write a motivation letter expressing your interest in this particular company and your **eagerness** to contribute to its success.

It's now time to worry about questions 5 and 6. Bear (*keep*) in mind that the only objective (*goal, aim, purpose*) of your correspondence is to pass the first **hurdle**, namely to be selected for a job interview. If you think the number of applicants with a profile similar to yours is very large, expect the person who opens your letter to look mainly (*primarily*) for reasons to put it on the rejection pile. Suppose there are one thousand replies. Then the person in charge of the selection will try to reduce this to a more manageable (*practicable*) number, say fifty applications. To eliminate nine hundred and fifty letters, very **coarse** (*crude, rough*) negative criteria will be used at this **stage**, e.g. the legibility of the letter and CV, spelling mistakes, age above or below preset limits, sex and/or **marital status**, minimum number of years of experience or higher education.

If you have any reason to assume the number of candidates will be very large, avoid giving details that might cause your application to land on the rejection heap, **proofread** your motivation letter and CV several times and have someone check (*verify*) them for spelling or grammatical mistakes (*errors*).

You might try a **trick** (*ploy, ruse*) to cause your letter to receive more attention than those of your competitors: delayed sending. There is of course the risk that it won't be examined at all, but if it is, chances are that the reader will no longer be in elimination mode and will notice positive points.

But the best way to have an **edge** on (*an advantage over*) your competitors is to send your letter and CV before the ad is published. How can you do that? You can do it by sending spontaneous (*unsolicited*) applications to companies you would like to work for, doing so at a time your application has a chance to **trigger** a positive reaction. There is no point in writing to a company in trouble, which is more likely to decrease than to increase its **staff**. By contrast, a company currently undergoing or planning changes is likely to show an interest in your spontaneous application if your profile has any relevance to its present or **forthcoming** challenges. To discover changes that are likely to (*will probably*) cause a company to look for new talent, use the Internet.

Forme du CV et de la lettre d'accompagnement

The above paragraph **underscores** (*underlines*) issues to consider when defining the content of the two documents materialising your application: your résumé, also called CV, your cover letter, also called motivation letter.

Before going any further, ask yourself what the reader wants to know and doesn't want or shouldn't want to know about you. Remember, this person is very busy and will not be pleased to learn about circumstances of your life or achievements you may be proud of but that have no relevance to the job you are applying for. Be careful, however, when **deemphasizing** portions of your life that are not in any way related to the coveted position. Don't eliminate them completely. A gap in a CV is suspect and may cause the reader to fear you might have spent in gaol (*behind bars, in prison*) the year between employer X and employer Y.

In line with considerations above, CV writing experts stress that persons involved in the selection process prefer CVs in reverse chronological order (so they can make sure the candidate is not an ex-**convict** (***gaolbird***)).

The problem with the chronological approach, however, is that you may have acquired the particular experience that best qualify you for the job at an earlier time. If such is the case, do not use the chronological order to list your achievements, list them by decreasing order of relevance to the job you are seeking, and include a brief paragraph called 'employment history', with month/year to month/year – name of employer – place (only city and country).

L'interview

Congratulations ! You've passed the first hurdle (*barrier, obstacle*). You are invited to an interview. Now how do you prepare for it? Again, suppose you were the interviewer instead of the interviewee and ask yourself how you would handle a dozen or so applicants. They already have undergone a pre-selection process based on the analysis of their letters and CVs, and have been ranked according to predefined criteria.

These documents give only an incomplete and maybe inaccurate (*fallacious, inexact*) image of the candidates. Incomplete, because they may lack important information. Inaccurate, because some may grossly exaggerate their own merits or even downright invent nonexistent characteristics or experience. Among the things that are difficult to discover by looking at their papers are candidates' social skills, their ability to perform under stress, their adaptability, their creativity, in other words, the set of characteristics that make up their personality. Not all job positions require or **rule out** (*exclude*) specific character traits, but most of them require some degree of certain natural dispositions.

The purpose of the interview, then, is on the one hand to check the **accuracy** (*truthfulness, exactitude*) of the claims (*statements, allegations*) in the CV and letter, and on the other hand to find out (*determine*) whether the candidate possesses a set of character traits that will contribute to his or her success in the job.

As a candidate, you should expect questions corresponding to these concerns and prepare for them. Be ready to substantiate (*demonstrate the **actuality** of*) positive points listed in your CV with **genuine** (*authentic*), interesting, and if possible verifiable details or anecdotes. Furthermore, try to find out in advance the character traits necessary for the coveted position (*the position longed for*) and imagine questions whose answers could reveal their presence. Desirable attributes are a function of the job itself and of your prospective employer. To learn about them, talk to people with experience of the job or knowledge of the company. And, of course, use the Internet.

Commentaires

Prononcez correctement !

...We would like to reach – *reach/rich*. Entraînez-vous à marquer la distinction entre voyelles longues/courtes : ***peach/pitch, sleet/slit,*** *read/**rid, bead/bid, treacle/trickle***.

...obtaining a job offer is akin to – *akin* est accentué sur la dernière syllabe, comme beaucoup de mots de deux syllabes commençant par *a* : *aboard, again, about,* ***aback, abreast,*** *ago, ahead, anew, across, around,* ***amiss, amidst,*** *apart, away,* ***awash, awry, ahoy***.

...defining the content – Le nom *content* (what is contained in something, e.g. *table of contents*) est accentué sur la première syllabe. L'adjectif et le verbe *content* (satisfied, satisfy) sont accentués sur la dernière syllabe. Autres exemples : *conduct* n, *conduct* v ; *contrast* n, *contrast* v ; *convert* n, *convert* v ; *convict* n, *convict* v, *present* n + a, *present* v.

...spent in gaol – L'orthographe américaine de *gaol* est ***jail***, également acceptée en Grande Bretagne et qui reflète mieux la prononciation.

Un homme averti en vaut deux !

...the person eventually hired – *eventually* (in the end, finally, sooner or later, at the end of the process) ne veut pas dire *éventuellement*, dont l'équivalent anglais est *possibly*. Même différence de sens entre éventuel et eventual. Curieusement, *éventualité* et *eventuality* ont exactement le même sens.

...reject your application – *application* (formal request for a job, a position, a distinction, a favour; it is presented by an *applicant*, who *applies* for the object of the application). Les mots *candidate*, *candidature* (US *candidacy*) s'emploient aussi, mais surtout pour des positions officielles (mayor, senator, president...) des titres académiques ou honorifiques.

...much more information – Le substantif *information* fait partie des *non-count nouns*, et est de ce fait toujours au singulier. Pour distinguer un ou plusieurs éléments situés dans un *non-count noun*, on utilise des expressions telles que *a piece of information, information items*. On dirait alors *many more information items* au lieu de *much more information*. L'anglais comporte un grand nombre de non-count nouns, et certains d'entre eux sont des *count nouns* dans un sens et des *non-count nouns* dans un autre. Par exemple, *time* : *time is money* (non-count) ; *he repeated his question several times* (count). Quelque autres *non-count nouns* : *intelligence, knowledge, patience, furniture, baggage, luggage, clothing,* ***footwear****, bread, milk, meat, air, hydrogen, sunshine, weather,* ***glue****, asphalt,* ***wool****, sugar,* ***corn***.

...privately owned or public – Dans ce contexte, *public* signifie *whose shares may be bought and sold by the public*. ***Public company*** se dit en français *société cotée*.

...of your correspondence – Remarquez le e au lieu du a dans le mot français homologue. Autres exemples: *absorbent, ambience, ambient, condescendence, consistence, independence, independently, insistence, insistent, persistence, persistent.* À l'inverse, le français exemple devient *example* en anglais.

...underscores (*underlines*) issues – Le sens de *issue* correspondant à celui du mot français est daté, voire périmé. An *issue* is a question, a problem, or the publication of a regular paper or magazine. *I read it in yesterday's issue of the Daily Mirror.*

...substantiate (*demonstrate the actuality of*) positive points – Le sens de actuality n'a rien à voir avec celui du français *actualité*, en anglais current events. Même remarque pour *actuel* et *actual* (real, factual as opposed to what is hoped for, dreamed about or **purported**).

À RETENIR Des mots qui vont très bien ensemble

...your educational background : the economic background, the political background, background music, to stay in the background.

...a potential customer : a prospective customer, a regular customer, a faithful customer, an awkward customer.

...from the buyer's perspective : from a new perspective, from another perspective, to put something into perspective, to open up new perspectives.

...advertising a job vacancy : a hotel vacancy (*an available room*), a job opening, a job opportunity.

...what type of organisation : an organisation chart, a non governmental organisation, a non-profit organisation, the World Health Organisation.

...chances are that the reader : to take a chance at something, by chance, a chance encounter, to have a chance to succeed.

...a chance to trigger a positive reaction : to trigger a debate, to trigger a riot (*an* ***upheaval****, an uproar*).

...In line with considerations above : in line with expectations, in line with the law, in line with forecast.

...You've passed the first hurdle : to clear a hurdle, the final hurdle, the main hurdle.

...your prospective employer : a prospective buyer, his prospective wife

Des passerelles

...people are ill at ease – De nombreuses expressions anglaises utilisent *ill* avec le même sens que des expressions françaises contenant *mal* ou *mauvais* : *ill at ease, ill humour, ill-humoured, ill-assorted, ill-conceived, ill-defined, ill-disposed, ill-treat v, ill-treatment, ill-gotten (ill-gotten goods never prosper).* Mais ***ill will*** (animosity, hostility) est plus négatif que *mauvaise volonté*, et ***goodwill*** (friendliness, kindness) a un sens plus large que *bonne volonté*. *Goodwill* est aussi le prix supplémentaire payé pour la réputation d'une firme que l'on rachète (en français *survaleur* ou *goodwill*).

...what type of organisation – La famille de mots *organise, organiser, organisation* a les mêmes sens en français et en anglais. L'anglais pour *organisateur, organisatrice* est *organiser*, et s est remplacé par *z* en anglais américain.

...the only objective (*goal, aim, purpose*) of your correspondence – Les mots correspond, correspondent, correspondence ont les mêmes sens que leurs homologues français, sauf lors des voyages, où une correspondance se dit *a connecting flight* ou *a connecting train*.

...the coveted position – Le mot *position* a tous les sens de son homologue français : *a ship's position, the enemy positions, a standing position, his position in society, a position in a company, France's position on tax havens*.

...even downright invent – *invent v, inventor, invention* : mêmes sens qu'en français.

Vocabulaire anglais/français

aback (take someone)	choquer, (prendre quelqu'un) de court
abreast	de front
accuracy	exactitude
actuality	réalité
ad (advertisement)	annonce
ahoy	ohé
akin to	de même nature que
amidst	au milieu de
amiss	qui ne va pas
applicant	candidat
application	candidature
awash	inondé
awkward for	incommode pour
awry	de travers
bead	perle
bid	offre
coarse	cru
complete (a sale)	réaliser (une vente)
convict	détenu
corn	maïs (US), blé (Angleterre), avoine (écosse)
credentials	qualifications
daunting	redoutable
deemphasize	accorder une moindre importance à
eagerness	empressement
edge	avantage
extoll	faire l'éloge de

eventually	finalement
footwear	chaussures, bottes, sandales, etc
forthcoming	à venir
gaol	prison
gaolbird	prisonnier
genuine	authentique
glue	colle
goodwill	bonnes dispositions, survaleur
hire	embaucher
hurdle	haie, obstacle
ill will	hostilité
inception	début, origine, création
jail	prison
job vacancy	poste disponible
look for	rechercher
marital status	situation matrimoniale
meet	faire la connaissance de
meet with	rencontrer
peach	pêche
pitch	poix, hauteur (du ton), tangage, discours pour convaincre (commerce, politique)
potential customer	client potentiel
proofread	relire
public company	société cotée
purport	prétendre
reach	atteindre, arriver à
require	nécessiter

rid	débarrasser
riot	émeute
rule out	exclure
shareholder	actionnaire
sleet	chute de neige fondante
slit	trancher
staff	personnel
stage	stade
stockholder	actionnaire
tentative	préliminaire
trade press	presse professionnelle
treacle	mélasse
trick . ploy . ruse	truc
trickle	ruisseler
trigger	déclencher
tweak	tordre, ajuster
underscore	souligner
upheaval	soulèvement
wool	laine

requirements (exigences)

goal, aim, purpose, objective

to avoid = éviter

relevance =

cover letter = motivation letter

above = ci dessus

below = en dessous

gap = trou

inaccurate : inexacte

Chapitre 2

Les trajets

Dans ce chapitre

- Trajets
- Vivre en ville ou à la campagne
- Covoiturage
- Télétravail

Une discussion sur les trajets

During a coffee-break, three people are **gathered** (*assembled*) around the coffee-machine: Eileen, a lively brunette who works in the accounting department, Thomas, an **intern** who recently moved from accounting for a one-month **stint** in sales, and Sabrina, in charge of customer relations.

Eileen :
– Hi Thomas, how are you doing today?

Thomas :
– Fine, Eileen, except my train was late and it was 9:20 when I arrived at the office. That's the problem when you live in a far-away (*remote*) **suburb** and work in town: you depend on public transports that are not always reliable. But it's not so bad, I can put up with it, my **internship** comes to an end (*will be over*) next month.

Sabrina :
– We'll miss you. But you'll have been lucky not to have to use a car like me. Living in the country, I have

to **contend** (*put up*) **with** a one-hour to one-and-a-half-hour **commute** twice a day.

Eileen :
– Yeah, you complain, but at least the air you breathe is clean and you wake up (*awake*) every morning to the music of **chirping** and **twittering** birds instead of traffic noise.

Sabrina :
– That's true. It's a choice, really. I miss some of the things the town has to offer, like good **movie-theaters**, chic department stores with the kind of clothes I like to wear, a variety of restaurants downtown and the architecture of houses in the old city center, but I love my garden and its surroundings.

Le pourquoi des trajets

A century or two ago, most of our **forebears** (*ancestors*, ***forefathers***) spent nearly all their lives in the village where they had first seen the light of day (*been born*). Farmers, labourers or craftsmen (*artisans*) resided and **toiled** (*worked hard*) in the same place. The **cobbler** repaired and made boots and other **footwear** in a workshop on the ground-floor of a small house that sheltered his family; the same could be said of the **blacksmith** who spent his days in the forge **hammering** out shoes and applying them to the hooves of neighbouring farms' horses; a mill **straddled** (*spanned*) a small river whose **gushing** (*rushing*, ***spurting***) waters moved a tall wheel that slowly turned a **grinding stone**. The **miller** lived there and supplied villagers with flour to bake bread once a week in the village oven. Other **landmarks** were the **wash house** bordering the river **upstream** of the mill, the church and its **graveyard**, and the pub. The village **catered to** (*provided for*) the main material and spiritual needs of its inhabitants. Visits to the nearest town took place on special occasions like a fair, or to buy items not available locally. Going farther afield was even rarer, except maybe for a **pilgrimage** or, in the case of young craftsmen, going from town to town to **hone** (*sharpen, improve*) their skills.

But in the nineteenth century, the advent (*arrival*) of engines powered by fossil fuels **unleashed** the industrial revolution, **fostering** (*encouraging the development of*) specialisation, trade, cheap and massive transportation of goods and people across land and sea, and gradually changed the placid ways of country life. Nowadays, a single farmer driving a tractor **produces** more food, albeit with the help of artificial fertilisers and pesticides, than a dozen farmers and labourers leading horses or **oxen** could obtain from the same surface a century ago.

Mechanisation freed country people to move to cities to live and work there or in factories (*plants*) on their **outskirts**. But these new opportunities proved unstable, and soon a great many workers could no longer find work in the vicinity of (*near*) their home, or an affordable home a short distance from work.

Today, this unbalance is widespread and affects people **in all walks of life**. Commuting, the modern term for daily **plying** (*going daily back and forth*) between work and home, is viewed as a normal state of affairs.

Remèdes classiques, limites et inconvénients

Since commuting has become a regular feature of modern life, political authorities have implemented solutions to make it happen on a larger scale, more smoothly and faster. They have enlarged roads, built networks of **motorways** leading to and around large cities as well as railway systems linking them to their immediate or extended suburbs.

Providing more transportation capacity on roads and rail reduces **traffic congestion**, but the necessary investments grow more costly as new lines or roads require expropriations across ever more densely populated areas.

Another limit is the resulting pollution, especially at peak commuting times when traffic slows down or comes to a **standstill**. Various approaches reduce the negative impact of road usage. One consists of providing efficient **mass transit** systems and enticing car owners to use them. Another is **car pooling**, in which several people travel together in the same car. Yet another is flexible working times, called flextime in the US and **flexitime** in the UK. Flexitime kills two birds with one stone: it reduces peak-time traffic and gives employees **leeway** (*freedom*) to combine professional activities with other aspects of their lives.

One of the most publicised measures to reduce traffic congestion and the associated pollution is the 'congestion charge' introduced by the first London Mayor Ken Livingstone after his election in 2000, as a solution to the seemingly (*apparently*) **intractable** (*unmanageable*) traffic problem in central London. According to the official Web site of the London government, 'Drivers in central London spent 50% of their time in queues, and every weekday morning, the equivalent of 25 busy motorway lanes of traffic tried to enter central London'. High resolution cameras now register car plate numbers entering or leaving central London and feed them to computers that compare them to a data base of authorised vehicles. Residents as well as some particular users are exempted, but for all others, the cost of driving a car there on weekdays between 7:00 a.m. and 6:00 p.m. is £8 per day. The scheme has resulted in a **dramatic** reduction of congestion as well as an increase in the use of public transport, and thus proven its value. However, few cities in the world have introduced congestion charges as yet (*so far*), among them Berlin, Cologne, Hanover, Milan, Singapore and Stockholm.

Des déplacements plus fluides et plus propres

More promising solutions are made possible by the electronic and digital technologies. The industrial revolution brought **sweeping** (*extensive*) changes but did so over several generations. Figures measuring high tech improvements from one decade to the next are **staggering**: the number of components on a chip, memory capacity and computing speed have been roughly doubling every couple of years since half a century ago, and they continue to increase exponentially. Advances in optics, electronics, communications and software bring about dramatic changes everywhere and in all aspects of our lives, including new ways to solve the commuting **conundrum** (*problem*, ***quandary***).

Car sharing and bicycle sharing systems are becoming commonplace. The general principle is to let users subscribe for a period such as a day, a month or a year. The user finds a vehicle directly or through the Internet, unlocks it with a special card that automatically triggers all necessary managing and controlling functions: recording the time and place, charging the user account etc. When the vehicle is no longer needed, the user parks it at the nearest station, in some cases at any authorised public parking place, making it available for another user. Pilot projects experimented with this approach a few decades ago, but it is now **coming of age** (*becoming fully established*). Such schemes are much more flexible than classic **car hire**. They reduce the number of vehicles parked or moving around, prompt some city dwellers to give up car ownership and improve the flow of traffic, for the mutual benefit of city residents as well as commuters.

Personal Rapid Transit systems are another, even more promising solution for moving people to and inside cities. In this concept, comparatively small and light cabins seating about 6 persons reach their individual destinations along narrow guide-ways, propelled by electric motors. Passengers board a cabin at one of a number of stations positioned alongside but apart from the guide-ways, so stationed cabins do not impede traffic flow. Users choose their destination and start immediately. Cabins are automatically directed towards their target station each time they pass a **switching** point in the network of guide-ways. Computers control the entire operation of the network and cabins, guiding cabins at switching points, keeping them at a safe distance from one another, slowing them down as needed, etc.

The concept was first implemented (*put in place*) in 1975 and is operating on the Morgan Town university campus in West Virginia. A PRT moves passengers to and from car parks at the Amsterdam/Schiphol airport, and a similar system will start operating shortly at London/Heathrow for the same purpose. An all-purpose version is planned to start operating at the end of 2009 in Masdar City, Abu Dhabi's post-petroleum city, where streets will be only frequented by **pedestrians** and cyclists.

Éviter les trajets complètement

A growing proportion of the workforce in any advanced country is either working in an office in front of a computer or visiting prospects, customers, suppliers or other contacts outside their organisation. In today's computerised, Internet-based world, none of these activities requires a physical presence on the **premises** of an organisation. Considerations of costs are no longer an obstacle to the new form of employer/employee relationship called '**telecommuting**' or '**telework**', where employees work from home at least a fraction of the workdays.

Telework is only practiced today by a minority of organisations, but several factors may cause it to spread:

- for employees, commuting time is wasted time which they could use to learn new skills, take care of their families or just enjoy life
- for employers, letting employees benefit from the advantages of telework is a way to motivate and retain the best
- for communities, telework means less need for costly investments in roads and transportation systems
- for the planet and for humans in general, it means less carbon dioxide emissions

In a not so distant future, governments might grant carbon credits to firms that let their employees work from home, city dwellers might start migrating back to villages, and new businesses might spring up in the country, where some people prefer to live and work. This movement has already started, but it is only a trickle, possibly the **bellwether of** (*the **harbinger** of, **heralding***) a complete reversal of the migration started in the nineteenth century.

Commentaires

Prononcez correctement !

...During a coffee-break – *break*: même prononciation que ***brake***. De même : *steak/**stake**, great/**grate***.

...chic department stores – *department*. Le suffixe ment ne modifie pas la position de l'accent tonique : *depart* → *department, defer* → *deferment, manage* → *management, merry* → *merriment, require* → *requirement.*

...but at least the air you breathe – *least* opposition syllabe longue/courte : *least/list*, ***bead/bid***, *cheap/*

chip, ***heal/hill***, *leave/live*, ***meal/mill***, ***reap/rip***, *steal/still*, ***wheat/wit***.

...clothes I like to wear – *wear.* Même prononciation que ***ware*** (pottery), et *where* en anglais britannique seulement : l'anglais américain fait précéder les mots *where, what, why, which* d'un son '*h*'. Lorsque *wh* est suivi de *o*, le *h* est prononcé comme s'il n'y avait pas de *w* : *who, whom,* ***whore*** (prostitute).

...a single farmer driving a tractor produces more food – *produces*. Utilisé comme verbe, produce est accentué sur la deuxième syllabe, comme substantif, sur la première : *farmers take their* ***produce*** *twice a week to the village market.* Autres exemples : *contact* v, *contact* n; *present* v, *present* n + a; *project* v, *project* n; *frequent* a, *frequent* v. Attention, ce n'est pas une règle générale : *concern* v + n, *control* v + n.

food. La double voyelle oo produit un son voisin de celui du français ou, long ou court. Son long : *food, mood, pool, cool, soon, smooth, root.* Son court : *foot, boot, cook, took, wool.*

...spent 50% of their time in queues – *queue* (people waiting in line) se prononce comme ***cue*** (signal to start).

...has resulted in a dramatic reduction – *dramatic.* Les mots se terminant par ic sont le plus souvent accentués sur l'avant-dernière syllabe : *historic, economic, patriotic, acerbic, mechanic* n, *monolithic,* ***pathetic***. *Mais histrionic, catholic, periodic.*

...have been roughly doubling – *rough*: *gh* se prononce comme un *f* : *rough, tough, enough*, (*ou* prononcé comme *u* dans *cut, tug, up*) *cough* (*ou* prononcé comme *o* dans *top, rob, rock*) ou bien ne se prononce pas : *high, height,* ***thigh***, *tight, light, thorough, although, through, eight, weigh, weight, thought.* Le chiffre eight se prononce comme *ate* (passé de *eat*). *Weight* se prononce comme *wait* n + v.

...possibly the bellwether of (*the harbinger of, heralding*) a complete reversal – ***wether*** (male castrated sheep), a deux homophones, *whether*, et *weather*. *Bellwether* (leading sheep with a bell round its neck).

PIÈGES À ÉVITER

Un homme averti en vaut deux !

...an intern who recently moved from accounting – Le mot qui oblige à employer le *simple past* et non le *present perfect* du verbe *move* est *recently*. En l'absence de ce mot, on dirait ... *an intern who has moved from accounting*. Le *present perfect* décrirait alors une situation présente, celle du stagiaire qui ne travaille plus à la comptabilité. Le simple past associé à recently met l'accent non sur un état présent, mais sur un mouvement passé.

...to contend (*put up*) with a one-hour to one-and-a-half-hour commute – Les traits d'union servent à fabriquer les adjectifs *one-hour to one-and-a-half-hour* qui décrivent *commute* et sont placés devant. Ils disparaissent dans la phrase *my commute lasts one hour to one and a half hour.*

...like good movie-theaters – Cette conversation a lieu entre des Américains, qui boivent du café plutôt que du thé pendant les pauses. C'est aussi pourquoi il est question de *movie-theaters* et non de *cinemas*, où l'on voit des *movies* et non des *films*. En outre, le mot *theatre* est écrit *theater*, et plus loin dans la même phrase apparaît le mot *center*, qui s'écrit *centre* en anglais britannique. Les mots anglais *litre, lustre, lacklustre, mitre, reconnoitre, spectre, calibre, fibre, sabre*, et *sombre* se terminent tous en *er* en anglais américain.

...the hooves of neighbouring farms' horses – *neighbouring* s'écrirait *neighboring* en anglais américain. Même différence d'écriture : *flavour, honour, harbour, armour, colour.*

...spiritual needs of its inhabitants – Les mots ***inhabit***, *inhabited, inhabitable, inhabitant* ont les mêmes sens que les mots français *habiter, habité, habitable, habitant*. L'anglais *inhabitable* a pour équivalent français habitable. Le français inhabitable a pour équivalent anglais ***uninhabitable***.

...networks of motorways – *motorway* (highway for fast traffic) en anglais britannique. Anglais américain : ***expressway, turnpike*** (expressway with toll).

...High resolution cameras – Le mot anglais *camera* a un sens plus large que son homologue français, et inclut les appareils photos.

... Advances in optics, electronics, communications and software bring about dramatic changes – dramatic (related to theatre, sudden and important). Le premier sens est le même que celui de *dramatique*, le second sens correspond au français *spectaculaire*).

...classic car hire – *car hire* anglais britannique, ***car rental*** anglais américain.

...a physical presence on the ***premises*** – Le mot anglais premise, au singulier, a le même sens que le français *prémisse*. Au pluriel, premises, il désigne le lieu où travaille un groupe de personnes appartenant à une institution ou une société.

Des mots qui vont très bien ensemble

...three people are gathered (*assembled*) around the coffee-machine : A coffee-break, a brand of coffee, a cup of coffee, coffee beans, **white coffee**, black coffee.

...It's a choice, really : A good choice, it's your choice, I don't have the choice, there is no other choice.

... flour to bake bread : A slice of bread, bread and butter, bread and water, the daily bread.

...unleashed the industrial revolution : To unleash passions, to unleash the dogs, to unleash violence.

...a regular feature of modern life- A regular occurrence, at regular intervals, a regular verb.

...The industrial revolution brought sweeping (*extensive*) changes : Sweeping changes, a sweeping statement.

...the bellwether (*harbinger*) of a complete reversal : *the bellwether* (an indicator of something), the bellwether of change. Au sens propre, *the bellwether* est le mouton porteur d'une cloche en tête du troupeau.

TRUC Des passerelles

...you depend on public transports – *transport* n, *transport* v ont tous les sens propres et figurés des mots français *transport, transporter.* Le mot anglais *transportation* est synonyme de transport au sens propre.

...unleashed the industrial revolution – Les mots *revolution, revolutionise, revolutionary* ont tous les sens des mots français *révolution, révolutionner, révolutionnaire.* L'anglais possède en plus le verbe ***revolve*** (move around an axis, spin, turn around).

...the placid ways of country life – *placid, placidity, placidly*: mêmes sens que les mots français correspondants.

...the necessary investments – *invest, investment, investor, investiture* ont les mêmes sens que leurs homologues français. Toutefois le sens militaire (investir une forteresse) de invest est désormais archaïque. On utilise à la place *surround.*

Vocabulaire anglais/français

bead	perle
bellwether	signe annonciateur
bid	offre
blacksmith	forgeron
brake	frein
car hire	location de voitures (anglais britannique)
car pooling	covoiturage
car rental	location de voitures (anglais américain)
car sharing	autopartage
cater to	satisfaire
chirp	pépier
cobbler	cordonnier
come of age (to)	arriver à maturité
commute n + v	trajet, se rendre au travail et en revenir
contend with	surmonter
conundrum	dilemme
cue	signal
dramatic	spectaculaire
expressway	autoroute (anglais américain)
flexitime	horaires flexibles
footwear	chaussures
forebear	ancêtre
forefather	ancêtre
foster	encourager
gather	rassembler
graveyard	cimetière

grate	râper
grinding stone	meule
gush	bouillonner
hammer	marteler
harbinger	signe annonciateur
heal	guérie
herald	annoncer
hill	colline
hone	affuter
in all walks of life	de toutes sortes
inhabit	habiter
intern	stagiaire
internship	stage
intractable	quasi insurmontable
landmark	repère
leeway	marge de manœuvre
mass transit	transports collectifs
meal	repas
mill	moulin
miller	meunier
motorway	autoroute
movie-theater	cinéma (anglais américain)
organic	biologique
outskirts	faubourgs
ox, pl. oxen	bœuf
pathetic	pitoyable
pedestrian	piéton
Personal Rapid Transit	Système PRT
pilgrimage	pèlerinage

ply	aller et venir
premise	prémisse
premises	locaux
produce	produit de l'agriculture
produce	produire
quandary	embarras
reap	récolter
revolve	tourner
rip	déchirer
setup	arrangement
spurt	jaillir
stagger	chanceler
stake	enjeu
standstill	arrêt
stint	passage
straddle	enjamber
suburb	banlieue
sweep	balayer
switch	aiguillage, aiguiller
telecommuting	travail à distance
telework	travail à distance
thigh	cuisse
toil	travailler dur
traffic congestion	embouteillages
turnpike	autoroute à péage (anglais américain)
twitter	gazouiller
uninhabitable	inhabitable
unleash	déchaîner
upstream	en amont

ware	poterie
wash house	lavoir
wether	mouton mâle castré
wheat	froment
white coffee	café au lait
whore	putain
wit	esprit

Chapitre 3

Réunions internes

Dans ce chapitre

- Utilité des réunions internes
- Divers types de réunion
- Conduite à tenir avant et pendant la réunion

Exemple de réunion

Participants are **department managers** at the regional office of a **sizeable** (*fairly large*) provider of **IT** services. They meet every Monday morning at 10 a.m. sharp (*at exactly 10 a.m.*) to review **ongoing projects** and discuss new business opportunities. John, as head (*chief*) of the regional office, **chairs** (*presides over*) the **meeting**. Other participants are Mohammed, who heads the group of personal computer and networking specialists; Elisabeth, whose team of object-oriented programmers participates in projects **requiring** a high **level** of technical expertise; Margaret, the sales manager; Patricia, who heads a large **pool** of programmers and analysts; and Alan, who **handles** budgets and **accounting** and closely **monitors** the costs **incurred** by (*associated with*) and the revenue **accrued** from (*resulting from*) each project.

John :
– Morning everyone, I'm **delighted** to see you all smiling and apparently in good shape. Today's **agenda** comprises two ongoing projects, Strawberry and Apple-tree, as well as an **RFP** (***request for***

proposal) on which we have decided to **bid** (*make an offer*).

As indicated in my e-mail about the agenda, Alan has **raised concerns** about project Strawberry's latest figures, and suggested we look for ways to keep its costs **within** its budgeted limits. Alan, can you please give us the facts?

Alan :
– Yes John. Programming expenses for phase two of the project **overshoot** (*exceed*) **forecasts** by 5%, and **acceptance tests** are not **completed** yet. Should **rework** be necessary, it might well **eat up** our profit margin.

Margaret :
– Before anyone thinks Patricia and her programmers are to blame (*to be held responsible*), let me state that the client has requested **belated** changes to a portion of the specifications agreed upon, causing **delays** and additional work. Circumstances such as this are covered by an unambiguous **provision** (*article, paragraph*) in the contract. We pointed it out to the customer when they requested the changes. We have presented them with an estimate of the corresponding (*associated*) price increase, which they approved and that we can use as base for additional invoicing.

John :
– That **settles** agenda point number one, then. Thank you Margaret. Now to point number two, about delays in project Apple-tree, managed by one of Elisabeth's experts. Elisabeth, will you please tell us more about it?

Elisabeth :
– John, the fact is we are in trouble and must do something to avoid further serious consequences. We have been missing two key project team members since the end of last month, and their absence has already caused significant damage. Jacqueline

Durham is on sick-leave and won't come back until the week after next. And as you know, Jonathan Smith recently had a skiing accident and broke a vertebrae, causing him to lie **flat** on his back in hospital for at least another month and a half. Both of them have specialised expertise not **available** in our regional office.

Margaret :
– This is **unfortunate**. We are **committed** (*we have pledged*) **to** complete the **assignment** on time and face **stiff** penalties should **completion** be postponed (*if completion is postponed*).

John :
– This **obviously** calls for immediate action. As soon as the meeting is over I'll phone Bob Smith of HRM (*human resource management*) at **head office** and sound (*query*) him about possible reinforcements. Elisabeth, please prepare a concise report on the status of the project, the required profiles and the reasons why you need them. It'll serve as ammunition to obtain the necessary assistance from our head office. Don't worry, they won't let us down. Appletree is a highly visible project, top management was involved in the final negotiation and knows the reputation of our company is **at stake**. Let's now look at our chances to get the order for project Hickory. Margaret, please explain the situation.

Margaret :
– Hickory falls into Mohammed's domain of responsibility and expertise, and we've already done a lot of work together on this project. The prospect wants to replace their entire network of personal computers with a **state-of-the-art** solution satisfying existing and **foreseeable** requirements regarding the availability and security of data and programs **throughout** the company. They have a large number of agents constantly moving around Europe, who need **seamless** and protected access to centralized data and applications as well as to their e-mails.

Mohammed :
– The solution we are proposing is based on the latest version of ABDC and guarantees a perfect integration of all network components. Systematic **data encryption** makes data **theft** or network intrusion **virtually** impossible. Applications will reside on central servers, which **obviates** (*renders unnecessary*) software updates on users' terminals. The only problem is the cost, as the solution calls for the replacement of a large number of hardware components that are now **outdated** and too slow to **cope with** forecasted **workloads**.

Alan :
– Do either of you know whether they are considering leasing the equipment?

Margaret :
– Not **to my knowledge**, but we'll discuss the project's financial aspects with the prospect this coming Friday and we'll review with them various ways of financing the operation.

John :
– What about competition?

Margaret :
– We know we are not alone. But we have two large users of ABDC among our clients, and both are extremely happy with the solution we have installed for them. Our competitors have practical experience with SOXA, but installed versions of that product do not offer as much data security as ABDC, and the new version is not yet available.

John :
– Let's keep our fingers crossed. **Keep me abreast** of any new developments on this front, and let me know if I can help you in any way. Thank you all for your contributions and comments.

À propos des réunions

There are many **kinds** (*sorts, varieties*) of meetings **depending on** the **size** of an organisation and the level at which the meeting is taking place. **Board meetings** held at the top of large **corporations** serve to establish or review (*examine, investigate*) **overall strategies**. A new strategy may **entail** (*imply*) **momentous** decisions with beneficial or **harmful** consequences for a company's various **stakeholders**: **shareholders**, clients, **suppliers**, employees and communities to which they **belong** (*which they are part of*).

At the other end of the spectrum you find smaller, less formal meetings in modest organisations, for instance a **weekly** meeting at group level. Their **purpose** may be simply to review and solve problems that **cropped up** (*appeared*) during the **previous** (*preceding*) week and assign tasks to participants for the **following** days. They are short and informal. For example it is rarely **deemed** (*considered, thought*) necessary to **write down minutes** and distribute them to participants.

For a meeting to be productive, participants should subscribe to its aims and cooperate to meet those aims. To **induce** cooperation, the chairperson should briefly remind participants, before **broaching** a new point on the agenda, of the pursued goals and of problems that need to be addressed (*treated, spoken about*). Participants should avoid attitudes or remarks that might **trigger** (*provoke*) confrontational reactions.

It is sometimes necessary to interrupt a speaker to ask for clarifications or **bring up** (*make, **utter***) at the right time an important comment or objection. The negative **impact** (*effect*) of interruptions should be **softened** (*reduced, attenuated*) by saying the speaker's name, thus **acknowledging** him or her, and using polite language, for example: 'Sorry to hold up the discussion, Jack, but if I may, I'd like to point out right now that there is absolutely no way the new product can be ready at the time mentioned in our plans.'

Commentaires

Prononcez correctement !

...a large pool of programmers – *Pool* contient un son de voyelle long comme *tool, mood,* ***moot, root****, boot, rule.* Des oreilles françaises peuvent confondre pool et pull.

... participates in projects – Beaucoup de mots de deux ou trois syllabes peuvent être des noms, comme ici, ou des verbes : *to project*. En tant que noms, ils sont accentués sur la première syllabe, et en tant que verbe, sur la dernière. Autres exemples : *conduct* n, *conduct* v; *contrast* n, *contrast*, v; *convict* n, *convict* v; *present* n or a, *present* v; *overshoot* n, *overshoot* v.

...overshoot forecasts... – *oo* dans *overshoot* est un son de voyelle long comme dans *boot, root,* ***stoop****, mood, moot, route, soup.* Le double *oo* produit souvent un son court, par exemple dans *foot, cook, book,* ***rook*** (a sort of **raven**, also a chess piece initially placed at opposite ends of the first rank), *took, should.* Dans le mot *blood, oo* est court également, mais produit le même son que *u* dans ***rug****, cut, rub,* ***tug***.

...unfortunate. – Les préfixes n'influent généralement pas sur la position de l'accent tonique. Ainsi : *fortunate* → *unfortunate;* ***praise*** → ***appraise****; way* → *away; cause* → *because; courage* → *encourage; pure* → *impure; understand* → *misunderstand*. Mais dans les mots utilisables comme noms ou comme verbes, le préfixe du nom peut être accentué comme dans *overshoot* n.

...employees – Tous les mots se terminant par ee sont accentués sur la dernière syllabe. Le suffixe ee correspond au é ou ée du participe passé français.

Ajouté à un verbe, il désigne une entité affectée par le verbe. Autre exemple : ***addressee*** (person to whom a letter is addressed), ***referee*** (person to whom one refers, a judge).

…right now – *right* possède deux homophones : le verbe *write* et le nom *rite* (same meanings as in French).

PIÈGES À ÉVITER

Un homme averti en vaut deux !

…this coming Friday – Les noms de jour et de mois sont des noms propres en anglais et prennent une majuscule. Leurs équivalents français sont traités comme des noms ordinaires. *He was born on a Sunday.* ***Grapes*** *are* ***harvested*** *from July to October in the Northern Hemisphere and from January to June in the Southern Hemisphere.*

…tests are not completed yet – L'adverbe *yet* lorsqu'il se traduit par *encore*, est placé en fin de proposition. Lorsqu'il est synonyme de *in spite of that, nevertheless*, il est placé en début de proposition : *She is old and sick, yet she continues to sing.*

…and her programmers – *Patricia's* programmers. Les accords en genre marchent de manières entièrement différentes en français et en anglais. Le choix de *her* au lieu de *his* veut dire que le possesseur d'une chose, en l'occurrence la personne responsable d'un groupe, est du genre féminin. Le pronom possessif français s'accorde avec le genre de l'entité possédée (*son* chien, *sa* voiture), quel que soit le genre du possesseur.

…committed to complete the assignment – *To complete* (to finish a task or an assignment). Ce mot possède un autre sens rappelant celui du verbe français, bien qu'un peu différent, dans l'expression *to complete a form*. On dit en français *remplir*, et non pas *compléter* un formulaire.

...at the top of large corporations – *corporation* (very large company with countless (*innumerable*) shareholders, typically listed on a **stock exchange**). Un sens bien différent de celui du français corporation.

...that need to be addressed – Dans *address* n + v, remarquez la double consonne, alors qu'il n'y en a qu'une en français. Autres exemples : *traffic, gallop, abbreviation, baggage, carrot, cotton. Exemples contraires : literature, literal, literary.*

Des mots qui vont très bien ensemble

... a large pool of programmers : A pool of talents, to **pool** resources, a swimming pool.

...has raised concerns : To raise an objection, to raise hopes, to raise false alarms, to raise a child, to raise chickens.

...serious consequences : To avoid consequences, to bear the consequences, to face the consequences, as a consequence of.

...less formal meetings : Board meeting, official meeting, the meeting place, an informal meeting, the minutes of a meeting, the agenda of the meeting.

...momentous decisions : A **fateful** decision, a courageous decision, a wise decision, a final decision, to reach a decision, to make a decision, the decision process.

...and solve problems : An insoluble problem, no problem, that's your (his, her, their) problem.

...confrontational reactions : Positive reactions, a negative reaction, an immediate reaction, a sudden reaction, a **knee-jerk** (*automatic, involuntary*) reaction.

Des passerelles

...a high level of technical expertise – *expert* (skilled and knowledgeable in a specialised area) et *expertise* (expert skill or knowledge in a specific field) ont une partie des sens de leurs homologues français. Pour les autres sens, les mots qui conviennent sont ***assessor*** (person who **assesses** something or someone, for instance ***insurance assessor***) et ***assessment*** (evaluation). Expertiser est en anglais *to assess*.

...of attention and discipline – Ces deux mots français sont des passerelles vers leurs équivalents anglais et les mots de même famille : *attention, attentionate, disciple, discipline, disciplinary.* Mais faire attention se dit en anglais *to pay attention.*

...ask for clarifications – *clear, clarify, clarity, clarification* ont les mêmes sens que leurs homologues français.

Vocabulaire anglais/français

acceptance test	test de réception
accounting	comptabilité
accrue	résulter
acknowledge	reconnaître la présence ou l'importance de
addressee	destinataire
agenda	ordre du jour (d'une réunion)
appraise	jauger, estimer
area	domaine
assess	estimer
assessment	estimation
assessor	expert
assignment	mission

at stake	en jeu
available	disponible
belated	en retard
belong	appartenir
bid n, v	proposition, faire une proposition
board meeting	réunion de direction
bring up	soulever (une question)
broach	aborder (un sujet)
chair	présider
commit to	s'engager à
committed	engagé
complete	achever
completion	achèvement
concern	souci
cope with	faire face à (une situation, une charge de travail)
corporation	grande société
crop up	surgir
data encryption	chiffrement des données
deem	considérer
delay	retard
delighted	ravi
department manager	chef de service
depending on	selon
eat up	dévorer
encryption	chiffrement
entail	entraîner, provoquer
fateful	crucial, grave
flat	à plat

following	suivant
forecast	prévision
foreseeable	prévisible
grape	raisin
handle	traiter
harmful	néfaste
harvest	vendange, moisson, récolte
harvest	vendanger, moissonner, récolter
head office	siège
impact	incidence
imply	impliquer
incur	entraîner
induce	inciter à
insurance assessor	expert d'assurance
IT (Information Technology)	technologie de l'information
keep abreast	se tenir au courant
keep (someone) abreast	tenir (quelqu'un) au courant
kind	sorte
knee-jerk	automatique
level	niveau
meeting	réunion
minutes	compte-rendu de réunion
momentous	lourd de conséquences
monitor	surveiller
moot	incertain, sujet à discussion
necessary evil	mal nécessaire
obviate	rendre inutile
obviously	évidemment

ongoing project	projet en cours
outdated	périmé
overall strategies	stratégies d'ensemble
overshoot	dépasser
pool	groupe
pool	regrouper, mettre en commun
praise	faire l'éloge de
previous	précédent (adj)
provision	article (d'un contrat)
pull	tirer
purpose	intention
raise	lever, soulever, élever
raven	corbeau
referee	arbitre
request for proposal	demande de proposition
require	avoir besoin de
rework	réfections
RFP	voir request for proposal
rook	freux (oiseau), tour (échecs)
root	racine
rug	couverture
seamless	sans à-coup
settle	régler
shareholder	actionnaire
size	dimension
sizeable	de grande dimension
soften	adoucir
stakeholder	partie prenante
state-of-the-art	à la pointe du progrès
stiff	sévère

stock exchange	bourse de valeurs
stoop	se pencher, s'abaisser
supplier	fournisseur
theft	vol
throughout	dans tout le (toute la)
to my knowledge	à ma connaissance
trigger	déclencher
tug	tirer brusquement, remorquer
unfortunate	malencontreux
utter	exprimer
virtually	pratiquement
weekly	hebdomadaire
within	à l'intérieur de
workload	charge de travail
write down	rédiger

Chapitre 4

La retraite

Dans ce chapitre

- Penser à sa retraite
- Une institution née avec la révolution industrielle
- Retraite par capitalisation ou par répartition
- Naissance et évolution des régimes de retraite

Exemple pratique d'indemnité de retraite

Any person who has worked in the USA, paid **contributions** to Social Security, worked a total number of years in the USA and elsewhere large enough to be **eligible**, receives **retirement benefits** after reaching retirement age.

Every year, Social Security sends the beneficiary an official document like this one:

***

Your New Benefit Amount

BENEFIARY'S NAME: GAIL M FORREST

- Your Social Security Benefits will increase by 5.8 percent in 2009 because of a rise in the cost of living.

<u>HOW MUCH WILL I GET AND WHEN?</u>

- Your new monthly amount (before deductions) is $114.00

- The amount we are deducting for Medicare medical **insurance** is $0.00

  (If you did not have Medicare as of Nov. 20, 2008, or if someone else pays your **premium**, we show $0.00)
- The amount we are deducting for your Medicare prescription drug plan is $0.00

  (If you did not elect withholding as of Nov. 1, 2008, we show $0.00)
- The amount we are deducting for US federal taxes is $29.10
- The amount we are deducting for voluntary federal **tax** withholding is $0.00

  (If you did not elect voluntary federal tax withholding as of Nov. 20, 2008, we show $0.00)
- After taking any other deductions, we will deposit into your bank account on Jan. 2, 2009, $84.90

If you disagree with any of these amounts, you should write to us within 60 days from the date you receive this letter. We would be happy to review the amounts.

***

This example shows two $0.00 withholdings (*deductions*) related to the US **health** insurance, for which the person is not eligible (*to which the person is not entitled*): Medicare, for health care **proper**, and the Medicare prescription drug plan, for medicines. Of the two lines regarding the U.S. federal taxes, one is always $0.00. In the case of a beneficiary who has not elected voluntary federal tax withholding, i.e. who does not declare revenues to the American tax authorities, as in the example, a federal tax of 25.51% is deducted.

La retraite et l'individu

Retirement is a subject some people don't worry about, since they are too busy and focused on the challenges and rewards of the present to think about such a remote (*distant, far-away*) part of their life. But in the minds of a large majority, retiring is the obligatory counterpart of working. Some don't enjoy working and find solace (*comfort, consolation*) in dreaming about the freedom (*latitude, leeway, liberty*) they'll enjoy once it's over for good, others like (*enjoy*) working and are wary of idleness and **boredom** (*ennui, dullness*) beyond their active life, yet others concentrate on financial aspects and make plans to live comfortably as retirees.

Confronted with the unknown, some will just hope for the best, others will think it makes it even more necessary to plan. Leaving aside catastrophic scenarios, a reasonable person could ask the following questions.

- At the time set for retirement, will I want to continue to work (*go on working*) and will it be possible?
- Conversely, will I want to retire earlier and will it be possible (*will it be an option*)?
- Where will I want to live once retired?
- When no longer active professionally but hopefully still physically and mentally healthy, how will I wish to spend my time?
- Where and how should I choose to live if and when my physical and possibly my mental health require special attention?
- How much money will I be able to spend every year after retirement?

La retraite, un problème de société

The amount of money available during retirement determines the degree of freedom in answering all other questions. This amount depends on many factors on which individuals have little control. In most advanced societies, planning for retirement is not left entirely to each person, contribution to a pension plan is enforced on both employers and employees, and rules and safeguards make sure abuse (*wrongdoings*), economic and other upheavals (*disruptions*) will not reduce retirees to poverty.

There are basically two mechanisms providing money to retirees. One is capitalisation, the other is **pay-as-you-go**. Both require contributions from workers, employees and often also the state, in other words the taxpayers. In the former approach, the money contributed is put aside and invested to build up capital available at retirement time. In the latter approach, the money contributed by employers and employees is used immediately to provide pensions to retirees.

The goal of both systems is to make sure retirees will indeed (*actually*) receive amounts that fairly correspond to the sums deducted from their earnings during their active life. The capitalisation system is favoured in Great Britain and in the USA, whose **pension funds** invest in securities (*stocks and bonds*) worldwide and play a major part in the long-term financing of the global (*wordwide*) economy. At least in theory, this system is immune to (*not affected by*) demographic fluctuations, as retirees will receive their pensions independently of the number of people at work. However, it is subject to variations in the value of investments. It has been tried with doubtful results in France before the first World War, when institutions managing capitalisation funds went bankrupt.

Pay-as-you-go systems, mostly used in Continental Europe, are not exposed to this kind of risk, but since pensions are paid by deductions from active workers' earnings, if the total amount of pensions increases (*goes up*), the total amount of deductions must also increase, even if there are fewer active people to support each retiree. When this happens, as it is all over Europe where people live longer and give birth to fewer children, several measures can prevent the system from breaking down (*collapsing*), none of which meets unanimous approval: increasing the rate of deductions, reducing pensions, raising retirement age, increasing immigration or finding ways to boost (*increase*) natality.

Genèse des systèmes de retraite modernes

Retirement systems were first invented for servants of the State. France created a retirement fund in 1673 for crews of its Royal Navy, and a similar institution was founded in 1768 in favour of all employees of the 'ferme générale', whose role was to collect taxes across the kingdom. The French Revolution then established a retirement system for all civil servants, later applied also to the military.

At the beginning of the nineteenth century, private sector workers started organising schemes called 'caisses de secours mutuel'. But each of these benefited only a defined category of workers. For instance, a 'caisse' was created for miners in 1894 and another in 1909 for state railway workers.

The first attempt at a general system for all categories of French workers is the 'retraites ouvrières et paysannes' created by law in 1910. The system, based on capitalisation, **collapsed** (*broke down*) as a result of the first World War, as subscribers were mobilised and could no longer pay contributions. It was replaced in 1930 by the 'assurances sociales', originally based on capitalisation, and later replaced by a pay-as-you-go system.

The earliest old age insurance system covering workers of all categories was instituted in 1889 in the German Reich by Bismarck. Contributions were **mandatory** (***compulsory***, *obligatory*). They were taken from employees as well as employers and supplemented by the state. The retirement age was initially set at 70 years. At the time, the life expectancy of a German worker was 72 years, so that a worker could expect to spend, on average, two years of his life in retirement. The retirement age was lowered to 65 years during the first World War. It has remained at this level for a long time, but according to a law voted in 2007 by the Bundestag it will be raised gradually to 67.

The German old age insurance system has survived two devastating wars, political upheavals, dictatorships as well as economic disasters. It is still operating (*working*) today on principles established more than a century ago. It served as a reference when Franklin D. Roosevelt established retirement funds within the framework of the Social Security Act in 1935, as part of the 'New Deal'.

La retraite dans l'avenir

Rules and systems governing pension schemes are based on a set of **assumptions** (*suppositions, hypotheses*) about work and the qualifications it requires, the successive stages of life, aging and its effects. These are no longer entirely valid.

Decades ago, a majority of jobs required physical strength, an attribute that still decreases with age but is much less in demand in our knowledge-based economy.

Until about fifteen years ago, the scientific community was convinced (*sure, certain*) that humans acquired new neurons until 24, then continuously lost more and more until death. This was **consistent** (*in agreement*) with a working life starting with learning, continuing with a productive stage in a given activity, followed by inexorable decline. The same pattern was thought to apply equally to activities demanding mental abilities as to those requiring physical strength.

The fairly recent discovery that **neurogenesis**, the process of forming new brain cells, continues throughout life, has abolished the dogma formerly associating aging with mental decline. We now know that healthy individuals can continue to learn, adapt to change and remain creative throughout their lives.

A number of baby boomers are already looking for alternatives to the traditional retirement pattern. Some do not want to retire at all, others would like to learn new jobs, yet others would prefer to work part time. The problem, however, is that the dogma of inevitable mental decline **endures** (*continues, persists*) outside of the scientific world. Employers are still determined to get rid of their aging personnel or refuse to grant them any special treatment.

Maybe realities will eventually become stronger than ignorance and **prejudice**. Maybe new life patterns will come to be adopted, with working periods alternating throughout life with periods where people learn additional skills or prepare to embrace (***take up***) entirely different professions.

Commentaires

Prononcez correctement !

...large enough to be eligible – *eligible*. Les suffixes *ible* et *able* n'influent pas sur le placement de l'accent tonique : *to digest* → *digestible, indigestible, horror* → *horrible, to believe* → *believable, unbelievable, to inhabit* → *inhabitable, uninhabitable, to elect* → *electable*. Certains mots terminés par ces suffixes ne dérivent pas clairement d'un autre mot, et dans ce cas l'accent est placé sur une syllabe antérieure : *eligible, formidable* ou *formidable*.

...Medicare, for health care proper – *health*. La combinaison de voyelles *ea* compte cinq prononciations : son bref identique à celui de *red, bed*, ***pet*** dans *breakfast, health, head, read* (passé de *read*) ; son *i* prolongé comme dans les mots contenant *ee* (*meet*, ***beet, steep***), dans *heal*, ***heap, peat, feat, reap***, *read* (infinitif de *read*) ; son diphtongué composé du son *i* suivi du son *e* de because dans *dear, fear, clear, near* ; son diphtongué composé du son *e* de *red* suivi du son *e* de the lorsqu'il est suivi d'un mot commençant par une consonne, dans *bear, tear, wear* ; son diphtongué composé du son *e* de *red* suivi du son *i* de *big* dans *steak, break*.

...retiring is the obligatory counterpart – *obligatory counterpart*. Plus les mots comportent de syllabes, plus il y a de chances qu'ils comportent un accent tonique principal (*primary stress*) et un accent tonique secondaire (*secundary stress*), lequel précède assez souvent l'accent tonique primaire : *unbelievable, economical, unavoidable, perspicacity, photographic*, mais pas toujours : *photograph secundary, necessary, obligatory, counterpart*. L'accent tonique principal n'est pas toujours au même endroit dans les mots de même racine : *economy, economical ; photograph, photographer, photographic* ; *catastrophe, catastrophic*. Notez que le *e* de *catastrophe* n'est pas un *e* muet mais se prononce comme dans la dernière syllabe de ***trophy***.

...money available during retirement *determines* – determines. Dans ce mot, la syllabe *mi* est non accentuée et se prononce comme la note de musique *mi* en français (et le *s* ajoute un son *z*). Dans le mot *undermine*, la syllabe *mi* comporte un accent tonique secondaire et de ce fait se prononce comme le possessif *my*.

... none of which meets *unanimous* approval – unanimous. Dans le dérivé *unanimity*, l'accent tonique est déplacé d'une syllabe vers la droite.

...each of these benefited only – *benefited*. Dans le dérivé *beneficial*, l'accent tonique est déplacé de deux syllabes vers la droite.

…and supplemented by the state – *supplement* n, *supplement* v, *supplemental* a.

…discovery that neurogenesis, the process of forming new brain cells – *neurogenesis*. Ce mot fait partie d'un ensemble de mots composés à partir de deux mots grecs dont le second comporte plus de deux syllabes. En pareil cas, la première syllabe du premier mot comporte un accent tonique secondaire, et l'une des syllabes du second, généralement la première, comporte l'accent tonique principal : *agoraphobia, endomorphism, idiosyncracy, metamorphose* v, *metamorphosis* n, *metempsychosis, metropolitan, microsurgery, microtechnique, monosyllable, nanotechnology, psychotherapy, thermonuclear.*

Un homme averti en vaut deux !

…for health care proper – *proper* (strictly so called). Placé après l'expression qualifiée, signifie *proprement dit(e)*. N'est pas synonyme de *clean*. Autres sens : *a proper job* (a real job); *a proper behaviour* (a suitable, an appropriate behaviour); *proper nouns*.

…how will I wish to spend my time – *time* correspond ici au français *temps*, comme dans l'expression *time is money*. Il correspond souvent à d'autres mots : *what time is it?, how many times have you gone* (been) *to England?*

…whose pension funds invest in securities – *securities*. Au singulier, *security*, ce mot a les mêmes sens que le français *sécurité*. Ici, au pluriel, *securities*, il désigne des titres, actions ou obligations, généralement cotées.

…later applied also to the military – *the military*. *The* + adjective désigne les membres d'un ensemble auxquels s'applique l'adjectif : *the poor, the dead, the blind, the innocent*. Ce sont des adjectifs pluriels (les adjectifs ne portent jamais la marque du pluriel), le nom est sous-entendu. Les mots français correspondants sont des noms au pluriel.

...humans acquired new neurons until 24 – *24*. En anglais, on ne précise pas qu'il s'agit de l'âge, alors que c'est nécessaire en français.

Des mots qui vont très bien ensemble

...contributions to Social Security : A social worker, social benefits, social graces (*polite and pleasant behaviour*), **social ladder**.

...for which the person is not eligible : Eligible for a discount, a highly eligible bachelor (*very suitable prospective husband*).

...beyond their active life : To save someone's life, a matter of life and death, life insurance, a friend for life, life expectancy.

...when my physical and possibly my mental health : Health insurance, health care, a firm's financial health.

...the long-term financing of the global economy : Global warming.

...according to a law voted in 2007 : Law and order, a law-abiding citizen, the rule of law, to break the law, the law of the jungle, to take the law into one's own hands.

... in our knowledge-based economy : Knowledge workers, scientific knowledge, knowledge management.

Des passerelles

...in the minds of a large majority – *A large majority, the silent majority, in the majority of cases, to attain the age of majority*, mêmes sens et mêmes constructions qu'en français.

...no longer active professionally – *To profess, professor, profession, profession of faith, the oldest profession, professional, professionalism*, une famille de mots et d'expressions parallèles dans les deux langues.

…will not reduce retirees to poverty – *Reduce, reduction, reducible* s'utilisent comme en français dans des domaines aussi variés que les mathématiques, la cuisine, les dépenses, les effectifs. Mais *irreducible* n'a pas le sens figuré du français *irréductible* (qui refuse de se rendre ou de changer d'avis).

…it will be raised gradually to 67 – Les mots *gradually, gradual* ont les mêmes sens que leurs homologues français. Ils dérivent de *grade*, mais ce mot a des sens différents dans les deux langues. ***Grade*** (a level of quality or size, a mark assessing the work of a student, a level corresponding to age or ability in a school system: *my daughter is in fifth grade*) n'a pas le sens du français *grade* dans les forces armées, qui se dit ***rank*** en anglais.

Vocabulaire anglais/français

assumption	supposition
beet	betterave
boredom	ennui
break down	s'effondrer
collapse	s'effondrer
compulsory	obligatoire
consistent (with)	en accord (avec)
contribution	cotisation
decade	décennie
eligible	qui à droit à
endure	se maintenir, continuer
feat	exploit
framework	cadre

grade	niveau de qualité
health	santé
heap	tas
insurance	assurance
mandatory	obligatoire
neurogenesis	neurogenèse
pay-as-you-go	par répartition
peat	tourbe
pension fund	fonds de pension
pet	animal domestique
prejudice	préjugé
premium	prime (d'assurance), cotisation
proper	proprement dit(e)
rank	grade
reap	récolter
retirement	retraite
retirement benefits	versements au titre de la retraite
securities	titres
social ladder	échelle sociale
steep	abrupt, très en pente
take up	se lancer dans
tax	impôt
trophy	trophée

Deuxième partie

À l'intérieur d'une organisation

Dans cette partie, vous verrez fonctionner certains rouages essentiels de toute organisation. Le chapitre 5, **Le téléphone**, contient d'utiles indications sur l'utilisation de cet outil dans le monde anglophone, le chapitre 6, **Rapports, mémos et e-mails**, est dédié aux trois formes les plus répandues de communication écrite interne et le chapitre 7, **La comptabilité**, évoque les documents et concepts essentiels de la comptabilité, indispensable à toute organisation professionnelle.

Chapitre 5

Le téléphone

Dans ce chapitre

- L'accueil téléphonique
- Quelques situations d'appel
- Surmonter les incompréhensions

La hot line du fournisseur de services Internet

You have signed up for the offer of Biggafone, a large telephone operator and **Internet service provider**, to provide you with high-speed Internet access and television through your telephone line in addition to voice transmission.

This is wonderful when it works, as it does most of the time. However, this **three-pronged** service requires the proper functioning of a long chain of components comprising the ISP's computers and their programs, the telephone line, the boxes connecting everything together, the proper connection of different cables, and in your computer, adequate parameters for programs that send and receive e-mails, let you surf on the Internet and protect you from hackers, viruses and other calamities. If one of the items in the chain breaks down or is maladjusted, you are deprived of one or all of the services you've paid for. When this happens, you first try to fix the problem by yourself, and as often as not (*fairly often*), you don't succeed. You then call up Biggafone's number. You are anxious (*eager*) to describe (*you are looking forward to describing*) your problem, but you must first listen to recorded information and instructions such as these:

> "Welcome to Biggafone.
>
> You will not be charged for the time until we put you through to your advisor.
>
> This call will be charged at the tariff of **a local call** if you call using one of Biggafone's fixed lines or our Internet telephone service. If you are interested in detailed information about this tariff, dial 9.
>
> For a malfunction, or for assistance with the installation or use of services provided by Biggafone, dial 1.
>
> For our offers, contracts, information about your invoice or the follow-up of your order, dial 2."

You don't want detailed info about the tariff (*list price*) of a local call, you just would like help to solve the problem at hand, so you dial 1, and the recording instructs you to:

> "Dial the ten digits of the fixed line for which you are calling our assistance service"

Having done so, you hear:

> "Have you thought of restarting your Biggabox by **unplugging** the electric cable from its socket and **plugging** it again? This simple manipulation often is enough (*suffices*) to solve a problem."

After this, there are three possibilities. If it's one of your lucky days, you can talk with a person immediately, but more often than not (*in the majority of cases*), you are advised of (*told about, informed about*) the approximate number of minutes you'll have to wait to start describing your problem. And if it's a bad day, you just hear another recording:

> "All our advisors are occupied (*busy*). Please call again later."

The problem is not that you **mind** (*are against, object to*) having to choose between options offered to you automatically. It is that presenting them via voice recordings is only possible sequentially and therefore slowly. Unlike a display of text and images presenting different options, like on an **ATM** (***automatic teller machine, cash dispenser***), where you identify instantly the option that matches (corresponds to) your particular need and press on it, voice recordings describe possibilities one by one. Moreover, the process is designed to work with everybody, not only with a normal person like you who is in a hurry, understands rather well and knows what she or he wants. Hence the initial comment to reassure an overanxious **caller** that there will be no charge for the waiting time, followed by an option to listen to details on the tariff of a local call.

Biggafone, whose raison d'être is to provide telephone services, knows full well (*perfectly well*) that the telephone is meant for interaction between humans. But it is big and wants to take advantage of its bigness to save (*economise*) on personnel costs. A trained switchboard operator can determine the motive of a call and assign it to the **relevant** (*appropriate*) specialised service in about 20 seconds if the caller is a normal person and maybe twice as long when dealing with a **moron** (*stupid individual*) or a person under stress. The robotised solution thus saves about half a minute of personnel costs per call, never mind that it **wastes** five minutes of client time. The time lost by clients does not cost Biggafone anything, at least in the short term, and as long as its competitors also disregard (*ignore, don't take into account*) the time lost by calling clients.

Conversations téléphoniques

The telephone is great (*very* ***convenient***) for any discussion with people we already know, because the sound of a familiar voice causes us to see a person **in our mind's eye**, which our memory and our imagination supply with an animated picture in keeping with (*reflecting*) the evolution and the tone of the conversation.

In professional life however, most phone conversations take place between persons who haven't met, but tacitly agree to speak together for a specific purpose. For the exchange to be satisfactory, something must be done to compensate for the fact that the talkers don't know and don't see each other. A ritual has emerged that applies equally to all kinds (*sorts*) of professions and situations. Following it **goes a long way towards** the efficient use of the telephone.

Répondre au téléphone

Anyone answering a call in a professional context should have three **goals** in mind:

- make a good first impression on the caller
- learn who is calling.
- identify the motive of the call

In the following sample answer, the person sitting next to a **ringing** phone smiles, lets it ring twice, then picks it up:

"Good afternoon, dental surgery John Smith, Doctor Smith's assistant Judith Barn speaking, how can I help you (*what can I do for you*)?"

The caller appreciates (*is glad*) not to have to wait more than two ringing tones, to be greeted by a smiling person, then have confirmation that he or she has reached the right place. The smile is not visible but is pictured in the caller's mind thanks to the friendly tone of the answer. Hearing Judith Barn give her first and second name, the caller might automatically do likewise (*do the same thing*).

From that moment on, the ice is broken. The exchange can proceed rapidly on a sound basis. If the caller **is in pain** after a recent intervention by Dr Smith, Judith might say:

"Please **hold on** a moment, Ms Breakwater, I'll ask Dr Smith"

Judith comes back with a tentative solution one minute later:

"Ms Breakwater? Thank you for holding (*waiting*). The doctor is with a patient and cannot take your call. He says your symptoms are typical of a wisdom tooth extraction and no cause for alarm. Take three tablets of Marstakin 500 as marked on your **prescription** and if it doesn't work for you, ring us again and the doctor will prescribe a more potent **painkiller** (***pain reliever***)."

Appeler

When initiating (*giving*) a call, the caller should always first return the **greetings** of whoever answers, then state the motive of the call in a polite and concise manner.

- "Good morning. I'd like to speak to Gerald Hammersmith. I'm a friend of his, Jim Bourgeois."
- "Good afternoon. My name is Mortimer Dupont. I'm writing an article for the Bonesticktown News about the proliferation of blackjack beetles in our county. I've heard about your success with organic products to eradicate some other **pests** and I need more detailed information on the subject. Could you please tell me who I might talk to?"

Déroulement et fin d'un échange téléphonique

Once a business conversation is initiated on the phone, it is important to bring it speedily (*rapidly*, ***swiftly***) to a positive conclusion for both sides. When the persons know each other, or are discussing a situation that is of interest for both parties, this goal is easily achieved. In other cases, the caller and his or her counterpart should strive at the initial **stage** of the call for (***endeavour*** *at the initial stage of the call to achieve*) a shared (*common*) understanding of its purpose. The conversation can then proceed smoothly, paying attention to a few simple rules.

- Be polite. Say please and/or use a modal such as *may I, could you please, would it be possible to, would you mind if we…*
- Make sure you understand and are understood. Factual data such as names, places, numbers can be securely exchanged, by repeating what you've heard to allow for correction, and if necessary, asking the other person to **spell** certain words: *I'm not sure I got it right, could you please say that again? And how do you spell (your, this, her, his, its, that) name? Could you please spell it for me?*
- Before ending the conversation, it is essential to recap its main points and results so that both parties memorise them in the same way. Otherwise, the exchange may do more harm than good, raising expectations that won't be fulfilled, **breeding** suspicion and rancour: *Good, so you'll e-mail us to confirm your agreement on a 10 percent rebate from your list price for a shipment of 58 broondicks to be delivered to our factory before the end of next month.* But this is not all. The calling party should thank the other party, say goodbye and wait for his or her goodbye in response before hanging up.

Surmonter la barrière des langues

All above recommendations **pertain** to telephone conversations between Anglophones. They should be followed even more by a person whose English is not yet up to par (*satisfactory, adequate, up to scratch*), with a particular emphasis on mutual understanding.

At each stage of the conversation, check your understanding by **acknowledging** what you've heard, repeating it in your own words and asking if it is what was meant. And if you don't understand a word, a phrase, a whole sentence, or if the person has **rattled** off (*spoken at great **speed***) a string of **utterances** (*words*) that make no sense to you, don't ever pretend you've understood (*don't ever do as if you had understood*). Don't ever hesitate (*never hesitate*) to say that you don't understand. You won't **lose** face. After all, it's not your fault if the other person speaks a language that takes (*requires, demands*) years of efforts to be perfectly understood instead of another that can be mastered in a few weeks or months, like Italian. Also, this person is certainly aware that you are not a native English speaker and should feel **compelled** (*obliged*) to facilitate your task. Here are some ways to obtain your counterpart's cooperation.

- I'm sorry to interrupt you, but I can't hear you very well, could you please speak up a little? (*could you speak a bit louder, please?*)
- No, it's not because we have a bad line. It's because I don't speak English well enough yet.
- I'm afraid I don't get (*understand*) what you've just said. Could you please repeat it, if possible using other (*different*) words?
- What word did you use after/before ***consignment***? Could you spell it for me?
- I'm still in the process of learning English. Would you mind speaking more slowly?

To spell difficult words, most people tend to use names of well-known places such as Paris or London or first names (*forenames*) such as John or Hubert. You might use instead the list known as *Nato phonetic alphabet*, which is in fact the *international alphabet for radiotelephony*:

Alpha, Bravo, Charlie, Delta, Echo, Foxtrot, Golf, Hotel, India, Juliet , Kilo, Lima, Mike, November, Oscar, Papa, Quebec, Romeo, Sierra, Tango, Uniform, Victor, Whiskey, X-ray, Yankee, Zulu.

Maybe it will help you to remember it all if you notice that this list contains six first names: *Charlie, Juliet, Mike, Oscar, Romeo, Victor; four places: India, Lima, Quebec, Sierra*; two dances: *Foxtrot, Tango*; two kinds of people: *Yankee, Zulu*; two Greek letters *Alpha, Delta*; and ten words without any affinities between them: *Bravo, Echo, Golf, Hotel, Kilo, November, Papa, Uniform, Whiskey, X-ray.*

Commentaires

Prononcez correctement !

...Biggafone, a large telephone operator – Attention à la position des accents toniques primaire et secondaires : *telephone operator.*

...one of the items in the chain breaks down – *A driver* ***brakes*** *to slow down his or her car. Breaks* et *brakes* sont des homophones, comme *steak* et *stake.*

...there are three possibilities – *possible, impossible* appartiennent à la même famille de mots mais sont accentués autrement que *possibilities.*

...options offered to you automatically – *automat, automatic, automatically.*

...hold on a moment, Ms Breakwater – *Ms* (*Ms.* en anglais américain) est la bonne façon de s'adresser à une personne de sexe féminin quand on ne sait pas (ou quand on ne veut pas montrer que l'on sait) s'il s'agit d'une femme non encore mariée ou d'une femme mariée, divorcée ou veuve (**widowed**), auquel cas la formule polie serait *Mrs Breakwater. Ms* se prononce d'une manière qui ressemble à *Miss*, en remplaçant le son s par un son *z*. *Mrs* se dit comme si le mot s'écrivait *Missez.*

...You won't lose face – Le *o* de *lose* (verbe) et le *oo* de ***loose*** (antonyme de l'adjectif *tight*) sont tous deux des sons longs, mais *lose* rime avec ***booze,***

snooze et *loose* rime avec ***moose*** (américain pour ***elk***) and *chocolate mousse*. (*Moose* et *mousse* sont homophones.)

PIÈGES À ÉVITER

Un homme averti en vaut deux !

...try to fix the problem by yourself – *problem* fait partie d'une longue liste de mots anglais avec les mêmes sens qu'un mot français, mais qui en diffèrent par l'absence d'un *e* final : *system, syntax, symptom, bard, cabal, optimist, visit, limit, citadel, violet, parallel, list.*

...detailed info about the tariff – Un certain nombre de mots ont une double consonne en anglais au lieu d'une seule en français : *tariff, address, gallop, carrot, traffic, baggage, abbreviation.*

...half a minute of personnel costs – Le nom *personnel* est ici ce qu'on appelle en anglais *a non-count noun* (comme *furniture, luggage, equipment, garbage* et beaucoup d'autres), synonyme de *staff.* L'équivalent de l'adjectif français personnel est *personal.*

...as long as its competitors also disregard – L'anglais possède toute une famille de mots pour rendre l'idée de compétition : *compete, competitor, competition, competitive, competitively, competitiveness, uncompetitive.* Ces mots s'utilisent dans n'importe quel contexte (sports, politique, affaires, biologie...). Le mot anglais *concurrent* (simultaneous, coincident, done or happening at the same time) est seulement un adjectif et son sens diffère de celui du français *concurrent.*

...hold on a moment, Ms Breakwater, I'll ask Dr Smith – *Ms, Mrs, Mr, Dr* s'écrivent *Ms., Mrs., Mr.* et *Dr.* en anglais américain.

...ring us again and the doctor will prescribe – *ring* au lieu de *call* en tant que verbe ou nom pour un appel téléphonique est de l'anglais britannique typique. Une américaine entendant *I'll give you a ring tomorrow* pourrait mal comprendre et espérer se voir offrir une bague.

...I've heard about your success with organic products – *I've heard* est le present perfect de hear. Le choix du *present perfect* au lieu du *simple past* indique que l'appelant ne se souvient pas – ou ne veut pas dire – quand ou dans quelle circonstance il en a entendu parler. Sinon il utiliserait le simple past : *Listening to the radio, I heard about your success.* En français nous utilisons le *passé composé*, qu'il y ait ou non une indication de circonstance ou de temps.

Des mots qui vont très bien ensemble

...it's one of your lucky days : *one of your lucky days, my salad days* (period of youthful inexperience), *in my student days, one of these days.*

...at least in the short term : *in the short term, in the long term* (in the long run).

...answering a call in a professional context : *a professional context, a professional attitude or behaviour, a professional football player, someone's professional expertise.*

...a more potent painkiller : *a painkiller, a serial killer, a killer application.*

...a positive conclusion for both sides : *a positive conclusion, a foregone conclusion* (inevitable result, decision made before the evidence is known), *to jump to conclusions* (make a hasty judgment or take a decision before knowing all the facts).

...you won't lose face : *to lose face, to lose one's reputation, nothing to lose.*

...because we have a bad line : *a bad line, a good line, in the same line of thought, our product line.*

Des passerelles

...as it does most of the time. – parallèle à notre expression *la plupart du temps*. De même, *time is money, I don't have the time, just in time.*

...there are three possibilities – *possible, impossible, possibility, impossibility*: mêmes sens que les mots français correspondants.

...whose raison d'être is to provide telephone services – *raison d'être* fait partie d'une longue liste d'expressions directement empruntées au français, dites à la française, utilisées avec le même sens dans les mêmes contextes. Beaucoup d'anglophones natifs n'ont même pas conscience qu'il s'agit d'un emprunt : *entre nous; the mot juste; to give someone carte blanche; an aide-mémoire; the maître d'hôtel; the savoir faire; a bon mot; the éminence grise; a fait accompli; a coup d'état; the coup de grâce; noblesse oblige; a femme fatale; de rigueur; a faux pas; comme il faut; comme ci, comme ça; après vous*; et bien d'autres.

Deux expressions extrêmement courantes sont absentes de cette liste car elles introduisent une connotation inexistante en français : *tête à tête*, et *rendez-vous*. Vous pourriez avoir rendez-vous avec votre pire ennemi pour tenter de régler un différent en tête à tête. *In English, if your wife has a rendezvous with her dentist, it can only be for a tête-à-tête that does not concern her teeth. If she tells you about it, she will use the word 'appointment'.*

...the sound of familiar voices – f*amily, familiar, familiarity, familiarise, familiarisation*: mêmes sens que les mots français correspondants.

...all kinds (*sorts*) of professions – *profession, professional, professionalism*: mêmes sens que les mots français homologues.

...the ice is broken – expression parallèle.

Vocabulaire anglais/français

acknowledge	confirmer la réception ou compréhension
ATM (automatic teller machine)	GAB (guichet automatique de banque)
booze	alcool (familier)
brake	frein, freiner
breed	susciter
caller	appelant
cash dispenser	automate bancaire
compel	obliger
consignment	lot (expédié)
convenient	commode
elk	renne (britannique)
endeavour	effort, s'efforcer
goal	but
greeting	salutation
hold on	rester en ligne
in one's mind's eye	dans son esprit
Internet Service Provider	fournisseur de services Internet
intersection	carrefour
local call	appel local
loose	lâche (contraire de serré)
lose	perdre
match	correspondance, correspondre
mind	esprit, faire attention à
moose	renne (américain)
moron	demeuré

pain reliever	médicament contre la douleur
painkiller	médicament contre la douleur
pertain	concerner
pest	insecte nuisible
plug	brancher
prescription	ordonnance
rattle	(faire) un bruit répétitif et saccadé
relevant	approprié
ring	anneau, sonnerie, téléphoner à (brit.)
snooze	somme, faire un somme
speed	vitesse
spell	épeler
stage	stade
swift	rapide
telly	télé
to be in pain	avoir mal
to go a long way towards	contribuer efficacement à
three-pronged	à trois volets (littéralement à trois dents de fourche)
TV	télé
unplug	débrancher
utterance	chose prononcée
waste	gaspillage, gaspiller
widow	veuve

Chapitre 6

Rapports, mémos et e-mails

Dans ce chapitre

- Rapports, mémos et e-mails
- Anglais formel ou informel
- Écueils à éviter

The preceding chapter dealt with business English spoken over the phone and **focused** on communication with outside contacts, as opposed to discussions among members of an organisation. By contrast, this chapter **pertains** (*is **dedicated***) to written documents circulating inside an organisation to guide or facilitate its operations. These are reports, memos and e-mails, all three abundantly used in most organisations. Reports and memos are by nature internal documents. E-mails are used both among members of the organisation and for communications with outsiders. In the latter case, they often replace letters, and have the same value as proof in the eventuality of litigation.

À propos des rapports

A report presents a higher echelon (*level*) of management with the results of a study, **survey**, research or other investigation conducted by a person or a group on a question of some importance on which decisions need (*have*) to be taken.

A report usually starts with a **reminder** of the circumstances that motivated (*caused*) the investigation, a mention of the contribution of each participant and a description of the resources and methodology used to find the facts it describes.
A key part of such a document is its middle part, which presents results, i.e. facts. Objectivity is **of the essence** (*critically important*), and some of the findings may be qualified with a degree of certainty or the mention of foreseeable developments that could invalidate them. The final part is a set of recommendations, i.e. practical steps that ought to (*should*) be taken **in view of** the realities reflected in the report.

A report should be as concise and clear as possible, but it always contains a large number of pages, which makes it impossible to insert a **meaningful** sample in this chapter.

À propos des mémos

Memos usually serve to disseminate information among groups larger than the **targets** of reports. Most often, responsibility for the contents of a memo is assumed by a single person, who is also its writer. Requirements of objectivity and concision are less **stringent** than for a report, but the information should be convincing and well presented. Memos are sometimes distributed via e-mail, but they are meant to be kept in printed form for **further** reference. **Actually**, *memo* is the abbreviation of Latin *memorandum*, which in English means *to be memorised*. The meaning is close to that of *aide-mémoire*, an informal document used in diplomatic circles. A memo is thus likely to survive much longer than transitory texts like e-mails, which justifies the time and effort invested in its preparation.

Exemple de mémo

Memorandum

From: Thomas Morelson, Bonesticktown **plant** director

To: All staff, Bonesticktown plant

Re: Sustainable development policies

All of you are aware of the risks a unit such as ours would present to the environment without all the safeguards (*precautions*) implemented (*put into effect*) before we started production three years ago. We went far beyond the minimal requirements set forth (*described*) in the charter for the preservation of the environment. For example, we recycle 90% of the water pumped out of the Frimostek River for our manufacturing processes and thus limit our water consumption to a tenth of our needs. As a result, our impact on the river is negligible compared with that of irrigation by farms bordering its **banks**. And our plant has never **leaked** toxic effluents, as evidenced by thriving **schools** of trout **downstream** of our site.

After discussing the matter with our personnel representatives, some of whom are **keen** nature lovers, we are now introducing new measures to further reduce our collective environmental **footprint**.

1) **Garbage** sorting.

Starting next month, you will notice coloured **bins** in the entrance halls of all our buildings. They will replace the larger green garbage containers whose contents have been so far taken weekly to Bonesticktown's **landfill**.

Plastic items, such as bottles, cups, etc. brought from outside or coming from vending machines on our **premises** should be dropped into the blue coloured bin marked 'plastic'.

Empty tins of soda, mineral water, fruit juice and other drinkable liquids are to be dropped into the white bin marked 'aluminium only'.

Cartons, magazines, newspapers as well as company documents **shredded** for confidentiality reasons are to go into the large yellow bin marked 'paper and carton'.

Glass objects are to be collected into the beige bin marked 'glass'.

All other items to be discarded should go into the green bin which will replace the larger green container. It is for miscellaneous garbage, with two notable exceptions.

a) **Batteries**. You will find, affixed to the wall, a red metallic box for used batteries of all kinds and sizes, which over time may leak toxic substances and are not meant to end up in a landfill.

b) **CFLs**. You have probably noticed that our maintenance has replaced incandescent light bulbs by CFLs (*compact fluorescent light bulbs*) in all our buildings. This represents an important saving and a major step in favour of the environment, as CFLs pay for themselves in about six months and dramatically reduce the overall emission of CO2 and other **harmful** substances. CFLs are not to be discarded with any other items, but must be taken to specialised recycling facilities that take care of the small yet hazardous quantity of mercury stored in them. As they are fragile (*breakable*), there is also a risk of breakage while installing or dismounting them. (Should you decide to install CFLs at home – a highly **commendable** (***laudable, praiseworthy***) option – you could ask Marjory Finnagan, in Maintenance, how to install or dismount a CFL without breaking it and what to do with a dismounted CFL.)

I count on your cooperation for properly **sorting out** discarded items. They will be taken once a month to the **relevant** (*appropriate*) regional recycling centres.

2) Bicycles, public transport and **car-pooling**.

Our car park comprises 70 **slots**, of which about 50 are currently occupied. The remaining capacity of 20 is not enough for the additional employees who will **join** us starting next September, should they need or chose to come by car. Extending the surface of the car park is possible, but expensive. The green faction among **employee representatives** made a few interesting suggestions. After careful review, they eventually matured into a viable alternative which will come into effect December 1st of this year.

As you know, all persons entering our premises, whether visitors or staff members, are subject to identity checks necessitated by the **sensitive** character of our activities. This makes it possible to **reward** those who make use of public transports or car pooling, or cycle to come to work. **Pedestrians**, car poolers and cyclists passing through the checkpoint will be handed special tickets, each of which will then be converted by **HRM** (***Human Resources Management***) into a £0.8 premium payable the following month.

This scheme, which is by nature voluntary, will mean more money for those who take advantage of it. It will reduce pollution and avoid the eye sore of a sprawling car park.

***

Exemple d'e-mail

To : Melanie Stringstop

From : Joe Philibert

Subject : Information request

Hello Melanie,

I've heard you worked on the Red-Penguin account back when you were down in our Sussex regional office. Could you spare a moment to chat on the phone? I am negotiating a new deal (*agreement, contract*) with them, and it would sure help a lot to hear about your experience with them, if you'll agree to share some of it with me.

Give me a call if and when your schedule permits (*your activities allow*). I'll be at my desk doing background (*office*) work all tomorrow afternoon.

Looking forward to talking with you.

Joe

Joseph Philibert, account manager

478 811 42 88

***

TEXTES

À propos des e-mails

E-mails are the least formal variety of written business (*professional*) communication. Writers use conversational English, with the degree of formality reflecting the type of relations they **entertain** with **recipients**. E-mails contain a short text often accompanied by one or several **attachments** of any kind (**spreadsheet**, presentation, picture, video or voice recording). They are normally sent to a single recipient and usually **address** only one issue (*question*), the so-called subject. Other persons are sometimes copied when the subject is **deemed** interesting for them (*of interest to them*), but a **downside** (***drawback***, *disadvantage*) of this practice is that people copied may feel obliged or entitled to participate in an exchange initially meant to remain **short-lived** and focused. This complicates the task of sender and recipient alike and translates into a costly loss of time for all people involved.

Properly used, e-mails can be a formidable means to enhance (*improve, reinforce, augment, increase*) the efficiency of an organisation. E-mails can be quickly answered (*replied to*) or forwarded to other recipients. Owing to their expected short **lifespan**, they are mostly kept only in digital form, which saves paper and ink, yet they can be retrieved almost immediately thanks to (*through*) content-based search functions of mail applications and operating systems.

They can foster (*encourage, develop*) teamwork, allowing people to ask colleagues with particular experience or knowledge for assistance or advice. They can **speed up** (*accelerate*) processes and increase an organisation's reactivity. They help put relevant information, e.g. via attached documents, in the hands of those who need it.

Unfortunately, e-mails are often misused. Some unnecessarily **inflate** the number of recipients, others always expect instant replies. A negative consequence is people constantly checking their smart phones for incoming e-mails instead of doing productive work.

Commentaires

Prononcez correctement !

...in the eventuality of litigation – *eventuality*. Accent tonique principal sur la syllabe a. (*Event, eventual, eventually.*)

...a reminder of the circumstances – *circumstances*. Accent tonique principal sur la syllabe *cir.*

...the resources and methodology – *methodology*. Accent tonique principal sur la syllabe *do*. (*Method, methodical, methodically.*)

...Memos usually serve to disseminate information – *disseminate*. Accent tonique principal sur la syllabe se. (Mais dissemination.)

...the abbreviation of Latin memorandum – *memorandum*. Accent tonique principal sur la syllabe *ran*.

...for our manufacturing processes – *processes*. Comme nom, *process* est accentué sur la première syllabe. Mais comme verbe, il est accentué sur la seconde : *to process*.

...our plant has never leaked toxic effluents – *leaked*. *A leak, to leak*, son long. Des oreilles françaises pourraient confondre *leak* (long) avec ***lick*** (court).

...as they are fragile – *fragile*. Le *i* est prononcé de manière à ce que *fragile* rime soit avec *angel*, soit avec *mile, pile, style*.

...Give me a call if and when your schedule permits – *schedule*. Les prononciations américaine et britannique sont très différentes. Britannique : comme les mots *shed* + *you'll*. Américaine: première syllabe comme celle de *skeleton*, seconde syllabe comme le début du mot *July*.

...and increase an organisation's reactivity – *reactivity*. L'accent tonique principal est sur la syllabe *ti*. Mais dans le verbe *react* l'accent tonique est sur *a*.

Un homme averti en vaut deux !

...A report presents a higher echelon (*level*) of management with the results of a study – Différence entre *present* en anglais et *présenter* en français : One presents someone *with* something. On présente quelque chose *à* quelqu'un. En anglais, le complément d'objet direct est la personne, en français, c'est la chose.

...steps that ought to (*should*) be taken in view of the realities – *in view of the realities* veut dire *as a result of the realities, taking the realities into account*. Les mots en vue de expriment une intention ou un but et sont rendus en anglais par ***with a view to*** : *she was saving money with a view to buy a car.*

...memo is the abbreviation of Latin *memorandum* – Latin: les noms des langues doivent obligatoirement commencer par une majuscule en anglais, mais pas en français. De même, les adjectifs dénotant une nationalité, une religion ou une origine doivent comporter une majuscule en anglais, mais non en français : *his Jewish father is Dutch and his Catholic mother is Italian.* Le mot *french*, que beaucoup de Français aiment écrire parce qu'ils pensent à tort qu'il indique leur nationalité ou désigne leur langue, ne peut s'écrire en anglais avec une minuscule que dans les expressions *french fries* et *french window* (porte-fenêtre). Partout ailleurs, *F* !

...as evidenced by thriving schools of trout – La langue anglaise comporte plus de mots spécialisés que le français pour les groupes d'animaux : *a school of fish, a **gaggle** of **geese**, a **flock** of birds, a **pride** of lions, a **herd** of cattle, a **pack** of hounds.*

...Empty tins of soda – L'équivalent américain de *tin* est ***can***.

...into the white bin marked 'aluminium only' – *aluminium.* Ce mot est accentué et s'écrit autrement en anglais américain : *aluminum.*

...CFLs – On forme le pluriel des acronymes en anglais en leur adjoignant un s: CFLs, CDs, CEOs. Même contraste avec le français pour les noms propres : *Yesterday we went out with the Duponts and they invited us for a drink at their place tomorrow to meet the Durands.*

...CFLs pay for themselves in about six months and dramatically reduce the emission of CO2 – *dramatic, dramatically* peuvent signifier *related to drama* comme les mots français correspondants. Mais leurs sens figurés sont différents. *Dramatic* veut dire *spectacular, sudden and impressive, **striking***.

...Our car park comprises 70 slots – *Car park* est l'équivalent britannique de l'américain *parking lot.*

…they eventually matured into a viable alternative – *eventual, eventually* synonymes de *final, finally*, ont un sens différent de *éventuel, éventuellement. Alternative* : signifie ici une autre solution que l'extension du parking. *An alternative* est ce qui remplace ou pourrait remplacer des choses ou des solutions existantes ou envisagées. Il peut y avoir plusieurs *alternatives* au sens anglais du mot. Une *alternative* est en français un ensemble de deux possibilités qui s'excluent mutuellement et entre lesquelles il faut choisir car il n'y en a pas d'autre.

…reflecting the type of relations they entertain with recipients – entertain dans ce contexte a le même sens que le français *entretenir des relations*. Mais *entertain* veut dire aussi *provide someone with amusement*, ou *receive people as guests and serve them food and/or drinks: the clown was entertaining the children; a beautiful country house where she likes to entertain friends and family*. Recipient: a person who receives something; *récipient* : un objet creux susceptible de contenir quelque chose.

…E-mails can be quickly answered (*replied to*) – *To answer e-mails*: *e-mails* complément d'objet direct de answer. En français, *répondre à des courriers électroniques*, complément d'objet indirect.

Des mots qui vont très bien ensemble

…steps that ought to (*should*) be taken in view of the realities : *in view of, with a view to, a room with a view, in my view* (in my opinion), *his political views*.

…After discussing the matter with our personnel representatives : *personnel representatives, a representative sample, the House of Representatives* (one of the two chambers of the United States Congress, the other being the Senate).

...avoid the eye sore of a sprawling car park : *an eye sore* (an unpleasant view). *A sight for sore eyes* (somebody one is pleased to see, a welcome visitor).

...e-mails can be a formidable means to enhance (*improve, reinforce, augment, increase*) the efficiency : *a formidable means; a means to an end; she is living beyond her means; by all means* (positive reply to person asking permission: *certainly, of course*); the ways and means.

...colleagues with particular experience or knowledge : *knowledge, knowledge workers, knowledge management.*

Des passerelles

...the information should be convincing and well presented – *presented*: Les sens de la famille de mots *present* n + a + v, *presentation, presentable, represent* sont les mêmes que ceux des mots *présent* n + a, *présenter, présentation, présentable, représenter.*

...you will find, affixed to the wall, a red metallic box – *metal, metallic, metallize, metallization* ont les mêmes sens que leurs homologues français.

...must be taken to specialised recycling facilities – *special, specialise, specialist, specialisation; cycle, recycle* ont les mêmes sens que les mots français correspondants. *Recyclage* est simplement *recycling.*

...this makes it possible to reward those – *possible, possibility, impossible, impossibility* ont le même sens que leurs homologues français. De plus, *possible* est l'équivalent anglais du français éventuel. Éventuellement n'a pas de traduction directe en anglais. On peut contourner la difficulté en utilisant un modal : *nous prendrons éventuellement un taxi pour y aller, we might take a cab to get there.*

...Writers use conversational English – *converse* v, *conversation, conversational* veulent dire la même chose que leurs homologues français. Mais *converse* a, n (something that is the reverse of a thing previously mentioned) n'est en français qu'une forme du verbe converser. L'adverbe *conversely* est l'équivalent exact du français *inversement*.

Vocabulaire anglais/français

actually	en fait
address	traiter
attachment	pièce jointe
bank	rive (d'une rivière)
battery	pile
bin	poubelle
can	boîte
car-pooling	covoiturage
CFL (compact fluorescent light bulb)	ampoule basse consommation
commendable	méritoire
dedicated to	destiné à, dédié à
deem	considérer comme
downside	inconvénient
downstream	en aval
drawback	inconvénient
employee representative	représentant du personnel
entertain	distraire, accueillir
eye sore	vue choquante par sa laideur
flock	groupe (d'oiseaux en vol)
focused	focalisé
footprint	empreinte
foreseeable	prévisible

further	ultérieur
gaggle (of geese)	troupeau (d'oies au sol)
garbage	ordures
goose (pl geese)	oie
harmful	nocif
herd	troupeau
HRM (Human Resources Management)	Gestion des Ressouves Humaines
inflate	gonfler
in view of	compte tenu de
join	rejoindre
keen	enthousiaste
landfill	décharge, déchetterie
laudable	méritoire
leak	laisser s'écouler
lick	lécher
lifespan	durée de vie
litigation	contentieux
loss	perte
meaningful	significatif
of the essence	fondamental
pack	meute
pedestrian	piéton
pertain to	concerner
plant	usine
praiseworthy	méritoire
premises	locaux
pride	famille (de lions)
recipient	destinataire
relevant	concerné, approprié

reminder	rappel
reward	récompenser
school	banc (de poissons)
sensitive	sensible
short-lived	de courte durée
shred	déchiqueter
slot	place (de parking)
sort out	trier
speed up	accélérer
spreadsheet	feuille de tableur
striking	frappant
stringent	strict
survey	enquête
target	cible
with a view to	en vue de

Chapitre 7

La comptabilité

Dans ce chapitre

- Rôle de la comptabilité
- Documents comptables
- Ratios
- Étapes d'évolution

À quoi sert la comptabilité

To plan the activities of an organisation in such a way that it prospers or at least is able to **pursue** (*continue*) its activities, the people in charge need information reflecting in some detail its **assets** (what it owns), its **liabilities** (what it owes), and the economic flows that have modified its assets and liabilities over a given period. Providing such information is the raison d'être of accounting.

To this end, **accounting** (***bookkeeping***) records each elementary operation of the business as it occurs, notes its value in a common monetary unit (***currency***), indicates its type (sale, purchase, payment made or received…) and various other attributes such as date, beneficiary, etc.

Accounting then processes these records to produce, among many others, two main documents: The **income statement** synthesises the activity of the organisation over a fixed length of time such as a month, a quarter or a year; the **balance sheet** shows the economic situation of the organisation at the end of the period. You will find these two documents in the annual report of any **listed** (*public*) company.

The income statement is constructed in the following way to explain the bottom line, i.e. the net income, a figure of particular interest to **shareholders** (***stockholders***) of the company:

Total revenue - **cost of revenue** (*cost of goods sold*) = **gross profit** (***margin***)

Operating expenses = research and development + cost of goods sold + **selling and general administrative expenses**

Gross profit - operating expenses = **operating income**

Operating income +/- other income and expenses = **earnings** before interest and taxes

Earnings before interest and taxes - interest = income before tax

Income before tax - income tax = net income

A balance sheet separately lists assets and liabilities, as in the following example:

ASSETS

Current assets

Cash 50,000.00	
Stocks and **bonds**	200,000.00
Accounts receivable	350,000.00
Inventory	100,000.00
Total current assets	700,000.00

Long-term assets

Building	300,000.00
Depreciation	(50,000.00)
Total long-term assets	250,000.00
Total assets	950,000.00

LIABILITIES

Current liabilities

Accounts payable	(100,000.00)
Mortgage payment	(50,000.00)
Total current liabilities	(150,000.00)
Long-term liabilities	
Mortgage balance	(200,000.00)
Total long-term liabilities	(200,000.00)
Total liabilities	(400,000.00)

Owner's equity = Total assets - Total liabilities
= $950,000.00 - $400,000.00 =
$550,000.00

Compte d'exploitation et bilan

Rubriques du compte d'exploitation

Revenue (***turnover***) includes goods and services sold during the accounting period. In the case of a manufacturing company, the cost of goods sold includes all personnel expenses (salaries, benefits…) **incurred** in manufacturing, as well as the cost of the parts that go into finished products. In the case of a **retail company**, the cost of goods sold will be the initial value of inventory, plus that of goods purchased, minus the value of inventory at the end of the period.

Selling and general administrative expenses include such items as **payroll expenses**, commissions, travel expenses for **executives** (*management*) as well as for the sales force, and advertising costs.

Rubriques du bilan

Current assets are the sum of cash and cash equivalents (money in the bank or safe (*secure*) and very liquid investments), accounts receivable, inventory, **marketable securities** (stocks and bonds), prepaid expenses, and any assets that could be converted to cash in less than one year.

Accounts receivable is money owed by **customers** (*clients*).

Long-term assets are a company's property (**real estate**, buildings), equipment (machinery) and other capital assets expected to be useable for more than one year, minus (*less*) depreciation.

By definition, current liabilities are **debts** a company must pay within a year. They include things such as mortgage payments, short-term **loans**, accounts payable, dividends and interest payable.

Accounts payable is money owed to **suppliers**.

Contrasting with short-term liabilities, long-term liabilities are due to be paid in more than a year. They may comprise mortgage loans, bank loans other than short term loans.

The owner's equity, the difference between assets and liabilities, is the value of the company, business or other entity. In the case of a listed (*public*) company, this difference represents the **book value** of the shares owned by stockholders. The shares' book value may widely differ from their value on the **stock market**.

Interprétation des documents financiers

Variations dans le temps

The income statement (*profit and loss account*) and the balance sheet of a business for a period such as the last fiscal year are interesting per se but do not give any idea about its evolution. This is why income statements and balance sheets usually display figures for several successive periods in adjacent columns. Sometimes the evolution from one period to the next is highlighted by successive percent changes for each row (*line*) in the statement.

Ratios élémentaires

The **current ratio** is the ratio of current assets to current liabilities. It gives a measure of a firm's ability to pays its short term debts. A ratio < 1 may indicate difficulties to meet obligations and thus a risk of **bankruptcy**, but not necessarily so. For example, if a firm's long-term prospects are outstanding, it might easily obtain loans to finance its present operations, an approach called **leverage**.

Other important ratios are the **inventory turnover**, or the ratio of the cost of goods sold to the average inventory; the **profit margin** (*operating profit margin, return on sales*), or ratio of the operating income to the revenue; the **equity ratio** or ratio of **owners' equity** to total assets; the **return on equity** (*ROE*), or ratio of net income to shareholder equity; the **price/ earning ratio** (*P/E*), or ratio of the price paid for a share to the net income per share.

La comptabilité hier, aujourd'hui et demain

Accounting may not be the oldest profession (***trade***, *metier, occupation*), but it is very ancient. Five millenaries ago, bookkeepers of Sumeria used **tokens** of **clay** and envelopes of the same material to record inventories (*stocks*) or transactions. This system later evolved into markings on tablets to indicate the nature of the goods. By 3000 BC, this symbolic representation had become the first known form of written language, allowing the Sumerians to record history and produce a written literature.

Coins appeared around 700 BC, further facilitating trade, and were key to the development of Greek and Roman civilisations. In the Middle Ages, villages were largely self-sufficient, but cities began to develop trade and the production of artefacts. The crusades **fostered** the development of trade with exotic goods from the East, practised primarily by Italian merchants. Around 1300 AD, they developed **double-entry bookkeeping**, in which each entry had a separate debit and credit.

The Industrial Revolution started in Britain in the 18th century and triggered (*led to*) another major accounting innovation, cost accounting. The name of a famous **potter**, Josiah Wedgwood, is closely associated with this discovery. Contrary to production by individual craftsmen (*artisans*), industrial production uses expensive (*costly*) machinery, and involves complex processes resulting in a number of different products. The cost accounting methods devised by Wedgwood allowed him to assess (*determine*) production costs for individual products. Armed with this knowledge (*information*), he could make vital decisions such as to cancel the production of goods that could not find buyers at a price above cost, and to concentrate his activity on goods with a higher profit margin.

The last stage in the evolution of accounting is closely linked to (*associated with*) the computer revolution. At negligible costs, computers collect data about individual transactions and process them to provide immediate answers to about any question a manager may ask before taking a decision.

The next stage is probably the application of sophisticated accounting and management techniques to ever smaller economic entities. The use of elaborate standard software such as data warehouse systems and so-called **enterprise software** is widespread in the corporate world. Such systems are comprehensive (*complete*), in the sense that they include all aspects of accounting, and adaptable enough to answer the needs of very different businesses. Less ambitious versions are now available to small businesses that run them on their own computers. The latest trend is software applications on demand running on the suppliers' servers and accessible via the Internet to users of any size.

Commentaires

Prononcez correctement !

...reflecting in some detail its assets (what it owns), its liabilities (what it owes) – *liable, liabilities*. Le suffixe ity provoque un déplacement de l'accent tonique principal. Autres exemples : *credible* → *credibility, probable* → *probability, possible* → *possibility, dual* → *duality, moral* → *morality, periodic* → *periodicity, senile* → *senility, valid* → *validity, virgin* → *virginity*. Notez que ity ne peut pas avoir le même effet sur les mots d'une syllabe, *scarce* → *scarcity, rare* → *rarity, vain* → *vanity*, car l'accent tonique tomberait alors sur le suffixe lui-même.

...accounting (*bookkeeping*) records each elementary operation – *element, elementary*. La terminaison *ary* provoque un décalage de l'accent tonique dans *element*, mais le plus souvent, l'accent tonique reste sur la même syllabe. Autres exemples : *illusion* → *illusionary; arbiter* → *arbitrary; moment* → *momentary*.

...successive percent changes for each row (*line*) in the statement. – Le nom *row* (line in a table) est prononcé comme le verbe ***row*** (propel a boat with oars), et comme le nom ***roe*** (one of two things: eggs taken from the ovaries of a fish or a kind of deer), des mots qui riment tous avec ***toe***, *snow, know, hollow*. The noun ***row*** (dispute, quarrel) est prononcé de telle manière qu'il rime avec *how, cow, now*. Deux autres mots de trois lettres en *ow* ont deux significations et deux prononciations différentes : le nom *bow* (weapon for shooting arrows) et le verbe ***sow*** (to plant seeds) riment avec *no, blow, crow, yellow*. Le verbe et nom *bow* (action of bending one's head in sign of respect), and ***sow*** (female pig), riment avec *now, ciao,* ***vow***.

...a measure of a firm's ability to pay its short-term debts. – Le *b* de *debt* est ignoré, et *debt* se prononce exactement comme le français *dette*. L'influence du français *débiteur* nous incite à prononcer le *b* de ***debtor***, ce qui serait une faute. *Debtor* se prononce comme s'il s'écrivait *dettor.*

...In the Middle Ages, villages were largely self-sufficient – *villages*. Dans les mots terminés par *age*, le *a* n'est pas accentué et se prononce comme le *i* bref de *bit, thick, bin*. Par exemple : *manage, savage, average, disparage, courage, garage*. Mais en anglais américain, ce dernier mot est accentué sur la syllabe *ra*: *garage*. Par suite, le premier a s'entend comme le *e* du français *que*, et le second *a* comme celui du français *âge*.

...The cost-accounting methods devised by Wedgwood – *methods*. Un *o* non accentué se prononce en général comme le *e* de l'article français le, mais si brièvement qu'il ressemble souvent à notre e muet, lequel ne s'entend qu'au sud de la Loire. Autres exemples : *Catholic, purpose, period.*

...Less ambitious versions – *versions*. La terminaison *sion* n'est jamais accentuée et se prononce comme l'adjectif français *jeune* quand elle est précédée par une voyelle : *collision, television, evasion, erosion*. Précédée d'une consonne, elle se prononce le plus souvent comme les quatre premières lettres du français *chenil* : *mansion, tension, pension, passion, torsion*. Quand cette consonne est un *r*, l'anglais hésite entre deux possibilités : *version* rime avec *television, immersion* rime soit avec *pension* (cas le plus fréquent), soit avec *television*.

Un homme averti en vaut deux !

...flows that have modified its assets and liabilities over a given period. – *period* est l'un des nombreux mots qui diffèrent d'un mot français par l'absence d'un *e* final : *method, problem, system, emblem, carbon, symptom, suffix, pilot, frontier, hymn, marmot, class, epithet, context. Period* comporte les sens du français période, plus celui du signe de ponctuation à la fin d'une phrase, aussi appelé ***full stop*** en anglais britannique.

...and various other attributes such as date, - *attribute* est l'un des quelques mots qui diffèrent d'un mot français par l'adjonction d'un *e* final : *jasmine, sense, chocolate, granite, future, case, compromise, profile.*

...two documents in the annual report – *report* est *rapport* en français. *Rapport* existe aussi en anglais mais signifie une relation positive avec une personne ou un petit groupe : *She had established a good rapport with her publisher.*

...the net income, a figure of particular interest to shareholders. – *figure* dans ce contexte a le même sens que le français *chiffre*. Ce mot désigne aussi l'aspect physique général d'une personne : *he's kept a boyish figure in spite of his age*. Dans ce sens, *figure* n'a pas d'équivalent français direct, sauf la traduction approximative *silhouette*, qui existe également en anglais. Le nom français *figure* désignant la partie antérieure de la tête se traduit par *face*. L'anglais *figure* v a les sens des verbes français *figurer* et *se figurer*. Au théâtre, on retrouve en anglais le mot *figurant*, qui se dit aussi *supernumerary actor.*

...= $950,000.00 - $400,000.00 = $550,000.00 – Les grands nombres sont présentés en anglais par groupes de trois chiffres (*figures*) séparés par une virgule (*comma*). Un point (*period, decimal point*) est placé entre les entiers (***integers***) et les fractions décimales. Dans le cas de montants d'argent, le symbole monétaire est placé directement devant le nombre.

...all personnel expenses (salaries, benefits...) – *benefit* (advantage or gift granted by an employer in addition to wages (*salaries*)). Contrairement au français *bénéfice*, l'anglais *benefit* ne peut s'appliquer à la différence entre les recettes et les dépenses, appelée *margin*, ou *profit*.

...In the case of a listed (*public*) company – *public* dans ce contexte désigne une société dont les actions peuvent être achetées ou vendues par tout membre du public sur une bourse de valeurs mobilières, par opposition à une société privée (*private company*) ou une société appartenant à l'état. A ***public company*** est une entité très différente de ce que nous entendons par *entreprise publique*.

...he could make vital decisions such as to cancel the production – cancel a des sens qui se recouvrent partiellement avec ceux du français *annuler*. *Cancel* ne convient pas (*is not the mot juste*) pour traduire *annuler* dans *annuler un mariage* ou *annuler le résultat d'une élection*. L'équivalent approprié est *to annul*. *Cancel* (marking a ticket or a postage stamp to show that it has been used) traduit *composter, oblitérer*. *To* ***obliterate*** (to destroy completely, to wipe out) et oblitérer sont des faux amis.

...The use of elaborate standard software such as data warehouse systems and so-called enterprise software is widespread in the corporate world. – L'adjectif *corporate* (relating to large companies or corporations) n'a pas d'équivalent français direct et s'utilise en français dans les milieux financiers. A *corporation* (a very large listed company) n'est jamais ce que nous appelons une corporation.

Des mots qui vont très bien ensemble

...all personnel expenses (salaries, benefits...) : *benefit, social benefits, the benefit of the doubt*.

...travel expenses for executives : *executive, the Chief Executive* (president of the United Sates), ***CEO (chief executive officer)***, *the executive branch of government* (as opposed to the *legislative branch* and *the judicial branch*), *an executive order* (in the USA, a rule issued by the president to a branch of government).

…assets that could be converted to cash : *cash. Cash and carry,* ***cash flow****, cash dispenser.*

…Long-term assets are a company's property (real estate, buildings) : *real estate.* ***Real-estate agent*** (***realtor*** in American English), *real estate agency.*

…the evolution from one period to the next : *evolution. The theory of evolution, the evolution of species, the evolution of the illness.*

…a risk of bankruptcy, : *bankruptcy, to face bankruptcy, bankruptcy proceedings.*

…if a firm's long-term prospects are outstanding : *prospects, disturbing prospects, encouraging prospects, prospects of recovery.*

...Coins appeared around 700, further facilitating trade, : *trade, the* ***trade press****, a* ***trade show****, a* ***trade union****, the* ***trade winds****.*

TRUC

Des passerelles

…The income statement synthesizes the activity – *synthesis, synthetic, synthesize* ont exactement les mêmes sens que les mots français correspondants. D'innombrables mots construits artificiellement à partir de racines grecques se retrouvent presque à l'identique dans les deux langues, avec exactement les mêmes sens. Le seul problème est l'emplacement de l'accent tonique : *synthesis, synthetic, synthesize.*

…You will find these two documents in the annual report – *document, documentation, documentary* a + n ont les mêmes sens que les mots français correspondants.

…figures for successive periods in adjacent columns. – *adjacent*: même sens que le mot français.

...This system later evolved into markings on tablets – *table, tablet* même sens que *table* et *tablette* en français. *Table* est aussi ce que nous appelons un *tableau* (format de données en informatique, ou une feuille de tableur). Ce que nous appelons tableau dans une salle de classe ou de conférence est selon le cas *a blackboard or a whiteboard.* Attention, un tableau papier se dit ***flip chart***. *Paperboard* est synonyme de ***cardboard*** ou *pasteboard.*

...another major accounting innovation – *innovate, innovation, innovator,* mêmes sens que les mots français homologues. L'adjectif *innovateur* (*trice*) a pour équivalent anglais *innovative.*

...concentrate his activity on goods with a higher profit margin. – *act* n + v, *actor, activity, action*: mêmes sens que les mots français correspondants. Mais ce que nous appelons *action* dans le contexte des marchés financiers se dit *share* ou *stock* en anglais.

Vocabulaire anglais/français

accounting	comptabilité
accounts payable	comptes clients
assets	actif
balance sheet	bilan
bankruptcy	faillite
bond	obligation
book value	valeur comptable
bookkeeping	comptabilité
building	bâtiment
cardboard	carton
cash	espèces
cash flow	marge brute d'autofinancement

CEO (chief executive officer)	directeur général
clay	argile
coin	pièce de monnaie
cost of revenue	prix de revient
currency	devise
current assets	actifs circulants
current ratio	ratio de liquidité
customer	client
debt	dette
debtor	débiteur
double-entry bookkeeping	comptabilité en partie double
earnings	gains
enterprise software	logiciels d'entreprise
equity ratio	ratio de l'indépendance financière
executive	dirigeant
flip chart	tableau papier
foster	favoriser
full stop	point final
gross profit	bénéfice brut
highlight	mettre en lumière
income statement	compte d'exploitation
incur	exposer (dépense)
integer	entier
inventory	stock
inventory turnover	rotation du stock
leverage	effet de levier
liabilities	passif
listed	cotée (entreprise, société)

loan	emprunt
long-term assets	immobilisations
margin	marge
marketable security	titres négociables
mortgage balance	dette hypothécaire à long terme
mortgage payment	dette hypothécaire à court terme
obliterate	détruire complètement
operating expenses	dépenses d'exploitation
operating income	bénéfice d'exploitation
owners' equity	fonds propres
payroll expenses	dépenses de personnel
potter	potier
price/earning ratio	PER ou quotient C/B (cours/ bénéfice par action)
profit margin	marge bénéficiaire
public company	société cotée
pursue	continuer, poursuivre
real estate	bien immobilier
real-estate agent	agent immobilier
realtor	agent immobilier
retail company	société de distribution
return on equity	rendement des capitaux propres
roe	œufs de poisson
row	ramer
row	rangée
row	querelle

selling and general administrative expenses	frais généraux
shareholder	actionnaire
sow	semer
sow	truie
stock market	marché d'actions
stockholder	actionnaire
stocks	actions
supplier	fournisseur
toe	orteil
token	jeton
trade	métier, échange
trade press	presse professionnelle
trade show	salon
trade union	syndicat
trade wind	alizé
turnover	chiffre d'affaires
vow	vœu, faire le vœu de

Troisième partie

Échanges et commerce

Cette partie vous présente en anglais des activités de communication et d'échange vitales pour la plupart des secteurs de l'économie. Au chapitre 8, **Présentations commerciales**, vous découvrez l'art de concevoir des présentations commerciales qui font vendre. Le chapitre 9, **Négociations**, illustre quelques principes essentiels de toute négociation. Le chapitre 10, **Distribution**, évoque divers aspects de la distribution. Le 11ème et dernier chapitre et du livre est consacré aux banques de détail, auxquelles ont recours toutes les professions.

Les deux premières parties vous ont familiarisé avec les commentaires, qui reprennent des fragments des textes anglais d'un chapitre pour illustrer des règles et des exceptions relatives à la prononciation ou à la grammaire, et des différences ou des ressemblances avec le français. Ces fragments et les autres exemples cités sont évidemment en anglais, mais les commentaires sont en français. Ce procédé comporte un avantage et un inconvénient. Il garantit la compréhension des explications mais vous oblige à passer constamment d'une langue à l'autre. La troisième partie vous dispense de l'effort intellectuel imposé par ce va-et-vient, en échange d'un effort pour comprendre les commentaires, désormais en anglais. La compréhension en est facilitée par l'adjonction de synonymes et par des renvois au lexique du chapitre, comme pour tout ce qui est en anglais dans l'ouvrage.

Chapitre 8

Présentations commerciales

Dans ce chapitre

- Parler ou écrire pour convaincre
- Les étapes d'une bonne argumentation
- Vendre à un client privé ou à une entreprise

Présentations commerciales à des particuliers

Many of us have a negative view of sales presentations, or sales pitches, as they are commonly called. The **phrase 'sales pitch'** brings to mind the door-to-door salesman who sold our grandmother her **vacuum cleaner**, the disruption of an interesting television programme by a series of advertising clips, or the intrusion on the phone by a telemarketer attempting (*trying*) to sell things we don't need and don't want.

Yet sales pitches are not made only by **obnoxious** people interfering with our private lives. We don't buy only goods or services. We also buy ideas, we get enlisted to defend a good cause or are converted to a new **faith** by people other than salespersons, who take us along the path from initial scepticism to **eventual** adhesion through the same tactics as our grandmother's vacuum-cleaner salesman.

Vous souvenez-vous de cet exemple d'argumentaire de vente ?

On an infinitely more modest scale, what is the introduction to this book, if not a sales pitch targeting you as a private buyer? It follows today's marketing experts' recommendations for sales pitches and commercial letters, with four steps already advised in the **time-honoured** AIDA method imagined by E.K. Strong in 1925 (nothing to do with a famous opera by Giuseppe Verdi).

A for <u>Attention</u>. The first page explodes the prevalent myth that 'learning English is easy' and asserts it is even harder (*more difficult*) for French speakers, calling the prospective buyer's attention to the severity of the problem.

I for <u>Interest</u>. The introduction explains convincingly why this is so and hints at the originality and **efficacy** of the book's approach.

D for <u>Desire</u>. A profile of potential readers reflects the hopes and frustrations of a vast majority who learned English at school, would like to practice what they've learnt but feel powerless when **confronted with** native speakers. Examples showing how the book helps overcome **stumbling blocks** cause them to crave (*yearn for, strongly desire*) the proficiency that has eluded them so far.

A for <u>Action</u>. The last paragraph entitled 'Et maintenant…' says each chapter can be read independently, so it's up to the reader to choose how to use the book. A choice obviously but tacitly **subject to** (***dependent on***) a buying decision. The last **sentence**, in English, is explicit: *And now, go for it!*

Any doubt regarding the merits of a sales pitch based on AIDA? Hey! You ARE reading the book, aren't you? And if you've come as far as its eighth chapter, chances are you've purchased (*bought*) it. As they say in English, the proof of the pudding is in the eating.

Argumentaires B2B

Sales pitches are not only used to generate sales in b2c (*b-to-c, business to consumer*) situations. They play a major part (*role*) in b2b (*b-to-b, business-to-business*) relations. Actually, the **stakes** are much higher in the wider context of business interplay (*interchange, interaction*). Grandma won't buy another vacuum cleaner any time soon, but an airline that has purchased a few planes from Airbus Industries is likely to buy more of the same model: it makes maintenance as well as training of pilots and **in-flight personnel** easier and less costly. New orders from an existing customer are called repeat business, requiring much less **strenuous** (*arduous*) sales efforts than new business (*first sales*). B2b suppliers therefore strive for (*try hard to establish*) long-term, continuously good relationships with existing customers, hoping for repeat business.

For all the above reasons, firms large and small in all branches of activity **devote** a lot of time, effort and money to get first orders from corporate prospects and medium-size or small companies.

Recommendations (*advice*) **pertaining to** (*concerning*) sales pitches aimed at individuals still apply, but the buying decision means a lot more for each side of a deal, making sales situations more complex. An order is not just the result of a brief interaction between a salesperson and an individual buyer, it is the **outcome** (*end result*) of a fairly long process involving several people on either side.

On the supplier side, there is always a salesperson, but higher echelons of management may be involved at one point or another, including the person at the top. The prospective client is usually represented by a member of the purchasing department, a counterpart of the salesperson (*the salesperson's* ***opposite number***).

But whereas the salesperson is – or should be – able to answer any question about the supplier's **product range**, its other clients, its position relative to competition, the use and benefits of its product or service, and to respond to any objection raised during a sales presentation, the purchasing department person's autonomy is limited. More often than not, other departments **participate in** the buying process.

A company may need to replace its air conditioning system, implement (*put in place*) a new computer application to automate one of its plants' production, select an agency for an advertising campaign or an architect to design its new headquarters. In all such cases, the buying decision is the result of internal interactions about the project, involving primarily one department in the role of the user, plus a few others in a technical or an **advisory** capacity. Users in the four cases above are respectively the human resources department, the manufacturing department, the sales and marketing department and the board of directors. Other participants may be IT, Finance, and the legal department. And the buyer's top executive usually has the final say in a project with a strategic impact.

The salesperson thus makes two kinds (*sorts*) of sales presentations: formal sales presentations to a group of persons representing various functions and interests, and informal sales pitches to individuals.

Commentaires

Prononcez correctement !

...sales presentations, or sales pitches – *sales* is pronounced exactly like (*is a homophone of*) *sails* (plural of ***sail*** n, or 2nd person of ***sail*** v). *Pitch*: Please do not confuse *pitch* with ***peach***. Similar risks of confusion *short vowel sound/long vowel sound:* ***bitch/ beach***, *rich/****reach***, *cock/coke, not/note*. However, ***poll*** and *pole* are homophones with both a long *o* sound as in *coke, note*. Same for ***roll*** and *role*.

…the path from initial *scepticism* to eventual adhesion – *scepticism* is spelled skepticism in American English. In both versions of English, the first syllable is pronounced like that of *skeleton*. Same for *sceptic, sceptical.*

…would like to practice what they've learnt – *would* and ***wood*** are homophones.

…Any doubt regarding the merits – *doubt* is pronounced to rime with *out,* ***rout, trout****:* the *b* is ignored. The same phenomenon occurs with *debt, debtor.*

…the proof of the pudding is in the eating – *proof*: long sound as in *roof, root, boot, ruse, blues*; *pudding*: short sound as in *put, took*.

…Actually, the stakes are much higher – *stakes* is a homophone of *steaks*.

…the outcome (*end result*) of a fairly long *process* – process: many two-syllable words are both a noun and a verb, and in most of them, the noun is emphasised (*stressed*) on the first syllable, whereas the verb is emphasised on the second syllable. *Process* n + v is one of the exceptions: ***processed cheese***.

…a project with a strategic impact – *project* n is stressed on the first syllable, *project* v is stressed on the second syllable. Other examples: *conduct* n, *conduct* v; *contrast* n, *contrast* v.

Un homme averti en vaut deux !

...an interesting television programme – *programme* is spelt *program* in American English. The spelling *program* is used also in British English in the context of IT (*information technology*). Similarly, *disk* is correct British English in *hard disk*, and *disc jockey* is the correct spelling on either side of the Atlantic.

...the originality and efficacy of the book's approach – The adjective *efficacious* is longer than its French equivalent *efficace*, and the noun *efficacy* is shorter than its French equivalent *efficacité*. The large number of French words ending in *ité* that have an English equivalent ending in *ity* might cause us to replace *efficacy* by a pseudo English word.

...but feel powerless when confronted with native speakers. – *confronted <u>with</u>*: the verb confront is used either with a direct object, e.g. *after reading this book, you'll be ready to confront native speakers, or with preposition with*. We say in French *être confronté <u>à</u>*, which might cause our erroneous use of the preposition *to*.

...the proficiency that has eluded them – *elude* has a general meaning similar to that of the French verb *éluder*, but the meanings do not completely overlap. We say *éluder des poursuivants*, ou *éluder une question*. In English you can say *to elude pursuers*, not a question. But the answer to a question may *elude you* (you: direct object). *A goal you are pursuing or are trying to achieve may elude you*. This construction is not possible in French, and *elude* cannot be translated using our verb *éluder*. A French equivalent of the **excerpt** could be: *l'aisance en anglais qu'ils ont vainement tenté d'acquérir*.

...the last sentence – *sentence* means the same in French and English when it refers to a punishment. In a grammatical context, the French translation for *sentence* is *phrase*. Note that the English noun *phrase* means ‘a small group of words inside a **clause**’ and has no direct French equivalent.

...strive for long-term, continuously good relationships – *continuously*: *continuous* and *continuously* are used when there are no interruptions in what is described by the adjective or adverb. The words ***continual*** and ***continually*** are used to describe things or conditions that occur very frequently: *she was attacked continually by mosquitoes during the night.*

...groups of persons representing various functions – *function* has the meanings of its French homologue fonction, plus that of an important ceremony: *he flew to London to attend a* ***function*** *commemorating a historic event.*

Des mots qui vont très bien ensemble

...sales pitches and commercial letters : *letters, a love letter, a letter of intent, a cover letter, a job application letter, a letter of application.*

...A profile of potential readers : *potential readers, potential customers, the potential energy, she has a lot of potential.*

...select an agency for an advertising campaign : *an advertising campaign, the presidential campaign, a campaign speech delivered before an election, a campaign event.*

Des passerelles

...a negative view of sales presentations – *present* a n v, *presenter, presentation* mean the same as *présent* a n, *présentateur, présentation* in French.

...the path from initial scepticism to eventual adhesion – *adhesion*, *adherent* a n, *adherence*, *adhere* v mean the same as *adhésion, adhérent(e), adhérence, adhérer* in French.

...what is the introduction to this book – *introduction, introduce, introductory* mean the same as *introduction, introduire, introductoire* in French.

...each chapter can be read independently – *independent, independence, independently* have the same meanings as *indépendant(e), indépendance, indépendamment* in French. The words *depend, dependent, dependence* also match the French words *dépendre, dépendant(e), dépendance*, apart from two differences: 1) we say in French *dépendre de, la dépendance de quelqu'un ou quelque chose*, whereas in English they say to ***depend on** or **upon** someone or something*; 2) *dependence* is not used to refer to a country that is subordinated to another, or to a smaller building or surface that is not physically attached to, yet is part of, a main property, as in the expression *une habitation d'une surface de 200 m² sans compter les dépendances.*

...good relationships with existing customers – *exist, existent, existence, existential* have exactly the same meanings as their French homologues.

...the purchasing department person's autonomy – *autonomy, autonomous*: same as *autonome, autonomie* in French. In addition, there is in English a matching adverb, *autonomously.*

...plus a few others in a technical or advisory capacity – *technical, technically, technique, technician*: same meanings as the corresponding French words.

Vocabulaire anglais/français

advisory	de conseil
beach	plage
bitch	chienne
clause	proposition (grammaire)

confronted with	confronté à
continual	continuel
continually	continuellement
continuous	continu
continuously	continûment, constamment
crave	désirer fortement
depend on or upon	dépendre de
dependent on or upon	dépendant de
devote	consacrer
efficacy	efficacité
elude	échapper
eventual	final
excerpt	extrait
faith	foi
function	cérémonie
in-flight personnel	personnel de bord
obnoxious	détestable
opposite number	homologue
outcome	résultat
participate in	participer à
peach	pêche
pertaining to	relatif à
pet	animal de compagnie
phrase	suite de quelques mots
poll	élection, enquête d'opinion
processed cheese	fromage fondu
product range	gamme de produits
reach	atteindre
roll	rouleau
rout	déroute

sail n	voile
sail v	aller en bateau
sales pitch	argumentaire de vente
sentence	phrase (grammaire)
stakes	enjeux
strenuous	pénible
stumbling block	pierre d'achoppement
subject to	subordonné à
time-honoured	consacré par l'usage
trout	truite
vacuum cleaner	aspirateur
wood	bois

Chapitre 9

Négociations

Dans ce chapitre

- Négociations internes
- Négociations avec des partenaires, clients ou fournisseurs
- Négociations avec des partenaires de différentes cultures
- Styles de négociation

Les négociations réduisent les incertitudes du futur en produisant des accords

Negotiations take place all the time whenever and wherever mutually accepted **rules** or habits have not determined beforehand (*in advance*) what is to be done. They **occur** between spouses, to take joint decisions about longer-term matters (*subjects*) such as whether to move to another region or country, how many children to have and how they will educate them, and on more immediate subjects such as who will **wash up** (*wash the dishes*) and who will **walk the dog**. In harmonious **households** (*families, ménages*), however, questions that otherwise might arise too often are **settled** once and for all. In the morning for instance, the male partner may get up before everybody and walk the dog before leaving for the office. His wife will take the children to school. And if some matters of mutual interest to children and parents are open to negotiation, others are better decided only by parents and imposed on children as ukases, with a view to teach them to respect legitimate authority and **abide by** (*act in accordance with*) the rules of civilised society.

Although professional life is more complex than family life, there are similarities. Inside an organisation, some day-to-day or long-term decisions are taken on the basis of authority only, others are taken after consulting the persons most directly concerned by them, yet others are the result of negotiations with groups or individuals. Salary rises (*increases*) may be linked to negotiations with **trade unions**, and an employee may negotiate a **rise**, a promotion, a **move** to another department or location.

But negotiations occur even more frequently with outsiders of an organisation. In fact, myriad (*innumerable*) daily transactions that are the lifeblood of businesses take place within the **framework** of previously negotiated agreements with outsiders: suppliers, large clients, banks, insurers, lawyers, advertising agents, government agencies.

The main purpose of all agreements, in business life as in private life, is to avoid having to negotiate all the time. Once a matter is settled in an agreement, there is no need to discuss it as long as the agreement endures. Agreements steady (*stabilise*) some important aspects of the professional environment. The **order book** of manufacturers such as aircraft manufacturers reflect negotiated agreements with their customers, allowing them to plan their production. **Conversely**, their customers need these agreements to plan the development of their own activities.

The example of airlines and aircraft manufacturers **hints at** (*indirectly alludes to*) a characteristic of any negotiated agreement, and **hence**, of all real negotiations: the outcome of a negotiation is an agreement if and only if all signatories benefit, more precisely, if for each signatory, the agreement is preferable to the absence of agreement. If a signatory **bows** to a deal that represents mainly drawbacks (*disadvantages*) and no benefits, it is not an agreement, it is a diktat. Historically, this kind of situation has been relatively frequent in relations among warring states, but examples also abound in economic life. The obvious goal of monopolies or cartels is to dictate prices and conditions to customers. A comparable situation is that of a **glut** (*plethora, overabundance*) of a given product, a condition called a buyer's market because buyers are in a position, if not to dictate prices, at least to cause them to be reduced dramatically. Conversely, a **dearth** (*shortage*) of something creates a seller's market in which prices and sellers' profits can go up enormously.

Dynamique de la négociation

The underlying assumption of a negotiation is that negotiating parties think there is a chance to benefit from a resulting agreement. This is a precondition for the start of any negotiation. The negotiation itself is a gradual exchange of information about each party's goals, priorities and main concerns. The respective goals, priorities and concerns are never fully compatible, so that each party has to give up (*renounce, abandon*) some of its own objectives to **accommodate** concerns of the other. There usually has to be some give and take on both sides of a negotiation for it to produce an agreement.

The willingness of a party to give more and to take less depends on how badly (*seriously*) it needs the agreement. An agreement is often more necessary or useful to one party than to the other. Experts on the dynamics of negotiation call the attention to what they call BATNA, or 'best alternative to no agreement'. If a partner's BATNA is catastrophic, it may cause it to make important concessions to avoid the catastrophe represented by a lack of agreement. An agreement must always be preferable for both parties than their respective BATNAs.

Before entering a negotiation, it is important not only to define one's goals and possible concessions, but also to gather information about the situation of the negotiating partner and to formulate hypotheses on its eagerness to conclude an agreement, the **alternatives** it might have, how it is likely to respond to demands voiced (*expressed*) during the negotiation and so on. As the negotiation proceeds, some hypotheses will be confirmed, others will **prove** erroneous, and entirely unsuspected information about the strategy and interests of the negotiating partner might be revealed. Or the negotiation will proceed without revealing much about the real situation and intentions of the other party.

Styles de négociation

The attitudes and behaviours of negotiators vary according to the mentality and skills of the individuals representing the parties concerned as well as to the extent of their mandate to negotiate. The relative size of each negotiating entity also plays a part. A person representing a powerful company might feel entitled to obtain more favourable terms from a smaller entity. On the other hand, a small company is more nimble (*agile*) and more adaptable than a large one, and the negotiator is more likely to be the ultimate decision maker. He or she may be more eager to secure the best possible deal and drive a harsher (*more ruthless*) negotiation than the representative of a large organisation.

In today's global economy, negotiations take place more and more between partners of different nationalities and cultures. Negotiators need to take cultural differences into account. For instance, Asian negotiators are less in a hurry to conclude a negotiation than their American counterparts, and tend to delay conclusion until an atmosphere of reciprocal trust (*confidence*) has been established. By contrast, a typical American businessman will put more emphasis on the solidity of the deal as guaranteed by a foolproof contract prepared by his firm's lawyers.

Commentaires

Prononcez correctement !

...decisions about longer-term matters (*subjects*) such as whether to move to another region of country – *whether* is a homophone of two other words: *weather*, and *wether* (castrated ram).

...before leaving for the office – *leaving*. Do not confuse *leaving* and *living*. Other examples: *heating*, ***hitting***; ***leaking***, *licking*; *peaking*, *picking*; *reaping*, ***ripping***; ***seeping***, ***sipping***; *sleeping*, ***slipping***; ***weeping***, ***whipping***.

...the rules of civilised society – *society*: *social* → *society*.

...there are similarities – *similarities*: *similar* → *similarity*.

...on the basis of authority only – *authority*: *author* → *authority*.

...cause them to be reduced dramatically – *dramatically*: *drama* → *dramatically*.

...if a signatory bows to a deal – *bows* is pronounced to rime with *cows*, ***vows***. Do not confuse this verb *bow* and the corresponding noun *bow* with the noun *bow* as in the phrase *bow and arrows*, that rime with *no*, *low*, ***blow***, ***sorrow***.

...The respective goals, priorities and concerns are never fully compatible – *compatible* → *compatibility*.

...according to the mentality and skills – *mentality*: *mental* → *mentality*.

...a typical American business man will put more emphasis on the solidity of the deal – *solidity*: *solid* → *solidity*.

PIÈGES À ÉVITER

Un homme averti en vaut deux !

...with a view to teach them to respect legitimate authority – 1) *with a view to*: the French equivalent is *en vue de*. *In view of* also exists in English, but with the meaning *because of, as a result of*: *in view of his illness, he did not go to work*. 2) *legitimate authority*. What is meant here is legitimate authority in general, therefore there is no article. But you would say *the legitimate authority of her parents*. Remember, when referring to something in general, no article: *authority, love, religion, philosophy*.

...Salary rises (*increases*) may be linked to negotiations – *rise* n is the British form of American ***raise*** n (in the particular case of salary increases).

...myriad (*innumerable*) daily transactions – *myriad* here is an adjective. This word may also be used as a noun, as in French: *a myriad of transactions*.

...The example of airlines and aircraft manufacturers – *example*: the e of this noun's French homologue *exemple* is replaced in English with *a*. The same substitution occurs with adjectives ending in *al*: *eventual, essential, formal, mortal, partial, venial*.

...Conversely, a dearth (*shortage*) of something creates a seller's market – *dearth*: in French, *pénurie*. The English ***penury*** refers only to the *extreme poverty* of a person and is not synonymous with *dearth*.

...each party has to give up (*renounce, abandon*) some of its own objectives to accommodate concerns of the other – *accommodate*: and *accommodation* mean the same as their French homologues in the field of vision. The meaning prepare as in *accommoder au beurre et aux fines herbes* does not exist in English, and the meaning *provide lodging* or *space for* does not exist in French.

...Before entering a negotiation – *enter* is a transitive verb in English.

...it is important not only to define one's goals and possible concessions – *possible* in this contexts is equivalent to French éventuel. This word can never translate *eventual* into French. *Éventuel* refers to something that might or might not occur. ***Eventual*** refers to something that will occur sooner or later or that will finally occur.

...how it is likely to respond to demands voiced – a *demand* is much more strongly expressed than *une demande* in French, the equivalent of which is *a request. Demand* may be translated by *exigence*.

...others will prove erroneous – *prove* has the same meaning as *prouver* in French, plus that of *turn out to be, be found to be*, in French *s'avérer.*

...and entirely unsuspected information – *information* is a non-count word, like *luggage, sugar, intelligence*. In most cases, the French equivalent of *information* (always singular) is *des informations* (plural). *Une information* : *an information item*.

...the extent of their mandate to negotiate – *mandate*: same meaning as a French word, with an e at the end, like *chocolate, compromise, debate, granite, jasmine, sense*.

...For instance, Asian negotiators are less in a hurry to conclude a negotiation than their American counterparts – *Asian, American*: In English, any part of speech specifying a geographical origin, a nationality, a language, a religious or philosophical belief require a capital letter. The parts of speech concerned by this rule are nouns, adjectives, verbs and adverbs. French grammar has a similar rule, but it concerns only one part of speech, namely nouns, and only those that indicate a nationality or geographical origin. We write: *C'est un Français, plus précisément un Bellifontain.* Et pour être encore plus précis, nous pourrions *écrire en français que c'était à l'origine un musulman de langue maternelle arabe et de culture politique marxiste, et que s'il a plus tard francisé son nom et embrassé la foi catholique, ce n'était pas en vue d'être traité plus chrétiennement par ses collègues français, mais seulement parce qu'il ne pouvait rien refuser à son épouse bretonne.* We would *write in* English *that he was originally a* Moslem *of* Arabic *native language and* Marxist *political culture, and that if he later* Frenchified *his name and embraced the* Catholic f*aith it was not with a view to being treated in a more* Christian *manner by his* French *colleagues, but only because he could not refuse his* Breton *spouse anything.*

Des mots qui vont très bien ensemble

...They occur between spouses, to take joint decisions : *joint decisions, a joint effort, a joint venture, a joint research centre.*

...Once a matter is settled in an agreement : *to settle a matter, to settle a dispute or a conflict, to settle a date; to settle* (establish a colony in) *a territory.*

...If a partner's BATNA is catastrophic : *a catastrophic outcome, a catastrophic scenario.*

...how it is likely to respond to demands voiced (*expressed*) during the negotiation : *to voice demands, to voice concerns, to voice objections, to voice one's opinion.*

...Negotiators need to take cultural differences into account : *cultural differences, a group's cultural identity, a cultural bias, a cultural event, cultural achievements.*

Des passerelles

...there are similarities – *similar, similarity, similarly*: same meanings as French *similaire, similarité, similairement*.

...if and only if all signatories benefit – *sign* v n, *signify, significant, signification, signature* n, *signatory*: same meanings as French *signe, signer, signifier, significatif, signification, signature, signataire*. In addition, *signature*, like most English nouns, may be used as an adjective, in which case it means *characteristic of a person or a thing*: *the chef's signature dish was a* ***casserole*** *of pheasant with* ***morels***.

...but example also abound in economic life – *abound, abundant, abundantly, abundance*: same meanings as French *abonder, abondant, abondamment, abondance*.

...A comparable situation is that of a glut – *compare, comparable, comparison, comparative*: same meanings as French *comparer, comparable, comparaison, comparatif*.

...An agreement is often more necessary or useful – *necessary, necessity, necessitate*: same meanings as French *nécessaire, nécessité, nécessiter*.

...some hypotheses will be confirmed – *hypothesis, hypothetical, hypothetically*: same meanings as French *hypothèse, hypothétique, hypothétiquement*. Many Greek words are used in both languages with the same meanings. Some of them keep (*retain*) their Greek form in English but not in French: *analysis, antithesis, basis, crisis, emphasis, hypothesis, synthesis, thesis*. The plural of these words is formed by replacing the ending *sis* with *ses* (pronounced *sez*): *analyses, antitheses, bases, crises, emphases, hypotheses, syntheses, theses*.

...A person representing a powerful company might feel entitled to obtain more favourable terms – *obtain, obtention, obtenable*: same meanings as French *obtenir, obtention, obtenable*.

Vocabulaire anglais/français

abide by	respecter (une loi)
accommodate	prendre en compte
alternative	autre possibilité
blow	coup
bow to	s'incliner devant
casserole	cassolette
conversely	inversement
dearth	pénurie
decision maker	décideur
entitled to	autorisé à
eventual	final
foolproof	à toute épreuve, sans faille
framework	cadre
glut	surabondance
hence	par suite
hint at	faire discrètement allusion à
hit	frapper
household	foyer, ménage
leak	fuir (liquide ou gaz)
morel	morille
move	mutation
nimble	agile
occur	se produire
order book	carnet de commandes
penury	grande misère
prove	s'avérer
raise (American English)	augmentation (de salaire)
rip	déchirer

rise (British English)	augmentation (de salaire)
rule	règle
secure	réussir à obtenir
seep	s'infilter (liquide)
settle	régler, décider
sip	siroter
skill	savoir faire, talent
slip	glisser
sorrow	chagrin
trade union	syndicat
vow	voeu, faire le vœu de
walk the dog	sortir le chien
wash up	faire la vaisselle
weep	pleurer
whip	fouet, fouetter

Chapitre 10

Distribution

Dans ce chapitre

- Évolution de la distribution au cours du temps
- Centres commerciaux extérieurs
- Réveil du centre ville
- La distribution et Internet

Conversation chez le quincaillier

Shop owner :
– Hello! What can I do for you today?

Customer :
– Hello, I'm not sure you have what I'm looking for, but on my last visit you **came up with** a brilliant solution and I thought…

Shop owner :
– Just tell me what you need and I'll see what we can do.

Customer :
– I'd like to buy a longer flexible shower **hose**. The one I have is all right to take a shower but I'd like to get one long enough to reach out to the **sink** (***washbasin***). I could wash the dog in it instead of doing it crouched or **kneeled down** next to the shower basin.

Shop owner :
– I see. Not a comfortable position, I wouldn't like that either. What length do you think you need?

Customer :
– The one that's installed is 150cm and it's too short. It should be at least 60cm longer to use the shower head from the sink.

Shop owner :
– That's too bad (*a pity*). There are only three standard lengths, 100cm, 150cm and 200cm. The only solution would be to attach two hoses together but for that you need a special kind of hose connector that I don't **carry**. You might **try your luck** at the Five-Season Mall. It's a 10 minute drive south on the M23 once you've left town. There you'll find a huge do-it-yourself shop called Fixit Hall where I assume they'll have that kind of contraption (*device*). I suggest you buy a 100cm hose from them and immediately check that the connector fits. You'll end up with a hose a bit (*somewhat*) longer than 2.5 metres. Do you need anything else?

Customer :
– Thanks for the advice. But yes, I'd like to buy kitchen **scales**. Do you have any?

Shop owner :
– Yep. I have several models. Do you have a particular use in mind?

Customer :
– Yes, actually (*in fact*) I cook with measuring cups and measuring spoons, which works fine with **recipes**, but I need to measure the dry food I **feed** my dog and my cat. The density of the dry food changes from one brand (*make*) to the next, so measuring glasses aren't practical (*convenient*). Rations are defined in grammes anyway and I'd like to weigh them each time.

Shop owner :
– Then I recommend this model. It's **sturdy** (*robust*), precise and very convenient. Just remove its plastic bowl and replace it with your pet's bowl or a container for whatever you need to weigh, then press the button on the left. The digital weight indicator

automatically sets itself to zero. You start **pouring** and stop once you've reached the desired weight, up to 5kg. Then use the weighed ingredients and forget about the scales. They switch themselves off automatically after a short while. This way they use very little current, which means you won't need to change the **battery** before a long time.

Customer :
– That sounds good. What's the price then?

Shop owner :
– $21.

Customer :
– OK, I'll take them. They seem much cheaper that some other models I've seen in the window of the **electrical appliance** shop on Main Street. Are you sure they'll last?

Shop owner :
– We've carried this article since the beginning of last year and we've sold a lot. We've had no complaints, so I assume (*suppose*) customers are very pleased with it. It's good value for your money. Anything else you'd like to buy?

Customer :
– No. That's all.

Shop owner :
– Will it be cash or charge?

Customer :
– Charge.

Shop owner :
– All right, please insert your card. You can type your code now. Here you are. Thanks for your visit. And if you go to Fixit Hall, please let me know how it goes. Good bye.

Customer :
– I sure will. Till next time, bye.

Centres commerciaux excentrés

Shopping malls (*shopping centres*) located outside of towns, like the one referred to in the above conversation, began to spread after World War II, first in the United-States in relation to the development of suburban living, then in Europe.

Goods and services are offered by large **department stores** as well as smaller shops **scattered** throughout the mall. The latter may be boutiques selling fashionable clothes or shoes, bookshops, hairdressers, wine merchants, bakers, delicatessens, **sweet shops**…. This combination of large and small retail businesses is comparable with that found in some city centres, but offers a wider choice and makes it possible to do all one's shopping on one single visit, without the **hassle** (*nuisance, annoyance*) of looking for a place to park or carrying things home by public transport. Furthermore, city centres, or downtown areas as they are called in the United States, also comprise offices and **flats**, so that their shops are more distant from one another than those of malls, making it impossible for shoppers to achieve as much in a single visit.

Commerces en ville

Concentrating a large variety of different retail businesses together in the same area is not a novel idea. Famous ancient examples are the covered bazaar of Istanbul first constructed in 1464 or the Iranian bazaar of Isfahan, which dates back to the seventeenth century. The Galleria Vittorio Emanuele II in Milan, built in the nineteenth century, is a magnificent covered arcade connecting the Piazza del Duomo to the Piazza della Scala.

What was new in the twentieth century is the creation of modern bazaars outside of cities, reachable (*accessible*) only by car. They make a lot of sense for people living in green suburban areas at some distance from a town. Rather than shopping in town, they drive to an extraneous mall where they find a comparable if not superior choice of shopping alternatives (*options*), while avoiding traffic jams and parking problems.

But far-away (*distant*) shopping centres do not improve the life of people living in a town. On the contrary, they reduce the number of their shopping options as some retailers opt to migrate to a shopping mall. Even worse, businesses that have moved away **henceforth** pay local taxes to other municipalities, depriving a city's government of resources to finance services used not only by its residents, but also by commuting suburban dwellers.

Vibrant (*dynamic*) modern cities act to reverse the migration of their inhabitants as well as of their retailing businesses. Improved public transports, extensive pedestrian areas, modern in-town shopping malls, networks of lanes reserved to cyclists and other schemes discouraging the use of cars in town all contribute to make urban life more interesting, more pleasant, and more convenient.

Achats sur Internet

The **advent** (*arrival*) of the automobile in the twentieth century brought significant changes to the organisation of retail in developed countries, but since the turn of the century, the computer revolution promises to have an even greater impact.

The Internet was hailed as **ushering in** (*introducing*) a new way to buy and sell as early as the 1980s, but it is only during the first decade of the twenty-first century that high-speed Internet access became as widespread everywhere as the automobile, accelerating the growth of Internet shopping.

Not all Internet users take advantage of the Internet to **complete** purchases formerly done only by visiting shops, but most of them gather information about products or services on the Internet before buying them. And if not all retail businesses sell via the Internet, a majority have a Web site providing information to clients and prospects. It is now common, even for small business entities such as independent wine merchants or restaurants to have an Internet site, as the cost of building and managing one keeps coming down.

Internet selling and buying are beneficial both to sellers and buyers.

Sales done via the Internet **obviate** (*eliminate*) or reduce a number of costs associated with sales through a shop: less **inventory**, no sales personnel, no need to rent or own (*possess*) space to welcome buyers. Whereas a brick-and-mortar **point of sale** only serves customers within a defined geographical area, there is no such limit in Internet selling.

Buying via the Internet offers the buyer a much wider choice and the potential to realise substantial savings: comparing prices and conditions is extremely easy, all the more so as comparisons can be done automatically by specialised sites.

Commentaires

Prononcez correctement !

...The one that's installed is 150cm and it's *too* short – too has two homophones: preposition *to* and number *two*.

...It should be at least 60cm longer – *least* has a long vowel sound, as opposed to *list* v n, which has a short vowel sound. Other examples: ***feast/fist***, *reach/rich*, *peach/****pitch***, *beach/****bitch***, *each/****itch***, ***teak****/tick*, ***seek/***

*sick, reed/**rid**, **beet**/bit, neat/**nit**, beat/bit, bean/bin, **wean**/win.*

...Do you have a particular use in mind? – *particular → particularity.* Ending *ity* causes the emphasis (*stress*) to move to the syllable preceding it. Other examples: *available → availability, responsible → responsibility, **promiscuous → promiscuity**, generous → generosity.*

...which works fine with recipes – *recipe*. There is a secondary stress on the last syllable *pe*, therefore it is pronounced like *pi* in *pity.*

...I'd like to weigh them each time – *weigh* is a homophone of *way.*

...You start pouring and stop once you've reached the desired weight – *pour* is a homophone of ***pore*** n v. These words rime with *more, store, core, door. Pore* as a noun has the same meaning as French *pore.* As a verb, it means to be absorbed in the study of something, usually a book: *he was poring over the Bible*. The adjective *poor* can also be pronounced like *pour,* but it is most often pronounced to rime with *moor* n v, *sure*. *Weight* is a homophone of *wait.*

...making it impossible for shoppers to *achieve* as much – achieve: the vast majority of words beginning with a are stressed on the syllable following the *a*: *among, about, administer, advice, arrive, ascribe, ashame, around,* ***appall*** (horrify), *American,* ***abet*** v. In most words beginning with a and stressed on their first syllable, the initial *a* is followed by two consonants: *acrimony address, adjective, African, advent*; but ***agony*** (pain, torment), ***alimony***.

...Internet selling and buying are beneficial both to sellers and buyers – *beneficial*: *benefit → beneficial.* Ending *cial, tial, ic, ical*, or *al* cause the placement of the stress on the syllable preceding them: *commerce → commercial, essence → essential, prudent → prudential, universe → universal, controversy → controversial, economy → economic, economical, catastrophe → catastrophic.*

...no sales personnel – *personnel*. This noun is stressed like its French equivalent. The position of the stress is what prevents a possible confusion with the adjective *personal*.

PIÈGES À ÉVITER

Un homme averti en vaut deux !

...It's a 10 minute drive – *10 minute*: *the drive lasts 10 minutes*. The phrase *10 minute drive* comprises a number and a plural noun, but as *10 minutes* is a modifier (*plays the part of an adjective*), the *s*, indicative of the plural, disappears. Reason: adjectives are invariable in English. Other example: the noun *trousers* is always plural, like other nouns of objects comprising two parts (*shorts, spectacles, scales...*), but when used as a modifier in front of another noun, trousers loses its *s*: *he put his wallet into his trouser pocket*.

...a hose a bit (*somewhat*) longer than 2.5 metres – *2.5*: About half the countries of the world use a decimal point as in English, and the other half use a decimal comma as in French. *Metre, centimetre, millimetre, kilometre* are spelt *meter* in American English. The word *meter* (a device for measuring) is the same in both versions; also *barometer, spectrometer...* Other words in *tre* in British English and *ter* in American English: *spectre, theatre, centre, mitre, lustre, calibre, fibre, sabre, litre, goitre*.

...I'd like to buy kitchen scales – *scales*: When it refers to an instrument for measuring weight, this word is plural, because the device was originally called a balance, comprised of two scales or pans, one on which to put the standard weights, and the other for what was to be weighed.

...Rations are defined in grammes anyway – *gramme* is the British spelling of American English gram.

...you won't need to change the battery before a long time – *battery* is the same word for what we call batterie and pile. **The former** is a *rechargeable battery*, **the latter** just a *battery*.

...the window of the electrical appliance shop – *the electrical appliance shop* (the shop selling electrical appliances). *Appliance* here is a plural noun, but as a modifier of *shop*, it does not bear a plural mark.

...boutiques selling fashionable clothes or shoes, bookshops, hairdressers, wine merchants, bakers, delicatessens, sweet shops – *bookshop* would be *bookstore* in American English; a *sweet shop* is a ***candy store*** in American English.

...city centres, or downtown areas as they are called in the United States, also comprise offices and flats – a *flat* is an *apartment* in American English.

...where they find a comparable if not superior choice of shopping alternatives – *alternative* has a different meaning than *alternative* in French, which means a set of two mutually exclusive possibilities. An *alternative* in English is just a possibility among several; *the alternative* is the other of two mutually exclusive possibilities. When asked towards the end of his long life how he felt about old age, John Kenneth Galbraith, the renowned Canadian economist and author of several best sellers among which *The Affluent Society* and *The New Industrial State*, replied (*answered*) that old age entailed a number of inconveniences, but he was absolutely convinced it was much preferable to the alternative. *Alternative* is also an adjective: *the alternative solution, an alternative solution*. But watch out (*beware*), *courant alternatif* is ***alternating current*** or *AC*, and *courant continu* is ***direct current*** or *DC*.

...less inventory, no sales personnel – *inventory* (list of goods in stock, or the goods in stock themselves). *Inventaire*, in French, only corresponds to the former definition.

Des mots qui vont très bien ensemble

...on my last visit you came up with a brilliant solution : *a brilliant solution, an easy solution, a simple solution, the best solution, a temporary solution.*

...I could wash the dog in it : *to wash the dog, to walk the dog, let sleeping dogs lie, it is raining cats and dogs.*

...You might try your luck at the Five-Season mall : *to try one's luck, good luck!, to be in luck, to be out of luck.*

...Concentrating a large variety of retail businesses together in the same area is not a novel idea : *a novel idea, a bad idea, a good idea, a bright idea.*

...while avoiding traffic jams and parking problems : *traffic jams, peak-traffic time, illegal traffic.*

...even for small business entities : *a small business, the Small Business Administration, business is business, business as usual, it's none of your business, mind your own business!, the business cycle* (recurring economic expansion and contraction), *a business plan, a business model, to mean business* (to be in earnest), *a business school.*

Des passerelles

...The density of the dry food changes from on brand (*make*) to the next – *density, dense*: same meanings as French homologues. Used informally, *dense* can also means *stupid*. It has a derivative that does not exist in French, the adverb *densely.*

...The digital weight indicator automatically sets itself to zero – *indicator, indicate, indication have the exact same meanings as indicateur, indiquer, indication. Automatically, automatic, automaton* (plural automata), *automate*: same meanings as French automatiquement, *automatique, automate, automatiser.*

...Then use the weighed ingredients – *ingredient*: same as *ingrédient*.

...Vibrant modern cities act to reverse the migration of their inhabitants – m*igration, migrate, emigrate, emigrant, immigrate, immigrant, emigration, immigration*: same meanings as the corresponding French words.

...the computer revolution promises to have an even greater impact – *revolution, revolutionary, revolutionise*: same meanings as French homologues.

...a majority have a Web site providing information – *information, inform, informant, disinformation*: same meanings as French *information, informer, informateur, désinformation*. But *information* is a collective noun in English, and as such is always singular. It is the usual equivalent of *des informations. Une information* is *a piece of information* or *an information item*.

...all the more so as comparisons can be done automatically – *comparison, compare, comparative, comparatively, comparator, comparable, incomparable*: same meanings as the corresponding French words.

Vocabulaire anglais/français

abet	inciter ou aider (à malfaire)
advent	venue, arrivée
agony	douleur intense
alimony	pension alimentaire
alternating current	courant alternatif
appall	horrifier
battery	pile
beet	betterave
bitch	chienne
candy store	confiserie
carry	avoir en magasin

come up with	fournir, produire
complete	effectuer
department store	grand magasin
direct current	courant continu
electrical appliance	appareil électrique
feast	festin
feed	nourrir (un animal)
fist	poing
flat	appartement
hassle	désagrément
henceforth	désormais
hose	tuyau
household	ménage, famille
inventory	inventaire, stock
itch	démanger, démangeaison
kneel down	s'agenouiller
nit	lente
obviate	rendre inutile
pellet	croquette (pour chien ou chat)
pitch	argumentaire, fréquence, poix
point of sale	point de vente
pore	se pencher sur, pore
pour	verser
promiscuity	rapports sexuels fréquents et indiscriminés
promiscuous	avec rapports sexuels fréquents et indiscriminés
recipe	recette
rid of	débarrasser de

scales	balance
scatter	éparpiller
seek	rechercher
shopping mall	centre commercial
sink	évier, lavabo
sturdy	robuste, solide
suburban	de banlieue
sweet shop	confiserie
teak	lteak (arbre)
the former	le premier
the latter	le second
toiletries	articles de toilette
try one's luck	tenter sa chance
usher in	introduire
washbasin	lavabo
wean	sevrer

Chapitre 11

À la banque

Dans ce chapitre

- Négocier un prêt
- Divers types de compte
- Internet et la banque

Discussion d'un prêt à l'agence locale de Hollyhock Bank

Branch manager :
– So Mr Kervill, you're applying for (*requesting*) a **loan** to boost your professional activities. I've looked at the history of your account since you became our customer two years ago, and **gathered** (*noticed*) that your income has grown steadily (*regularly*) if rather slowly over the last two years. I've also read **Puppy** Housebreaking Ltd's business plan. Before we discuss this question of loan, let me **congratulate** you on your idea to offer dog owners **housetraining** services. I like the way you've converted a widespread yet **unmet** need into a business opportunity. Based on my experience with dogs, I imagine many puppy owners would gladly spend money to alleviate their **housebreaking** problem (*to reduce the severity of their housebreaking problem*).

Jonathan Kervill :
– And in return, let me compliment your bank for having chosen for its name one of my preferred flowers and **appointed** a charming young lady as a

branch manager. What a refreshing change from the traditional banking business with its **stuffy** old-boy network of cigar-smoking smart alecks (*know-it-alls, wise guys, smart asses*) who've wrecked (*demolished, destroyed*) the global (*world*) economy (*brought the world economy to its knees*)!

Judith Bakerwolt :
– Thank you for appreciating that **Hollyhock** is not like most other banks, Mr Kervill. We strive (*try hard*) to better understand our customers so as to provide them with the best possible financial assistance. But when checking the creditworthiness of loan applicants, we are as meticulous as any other bank, even more so, actually (*in fact*). We consult credit **rating agencies** and carefully calculate credit scores. This is done by a department of our headquarters that even initiates additional investigations in some cases. But once this is done, granting a loan or rejecting an application is always the sole (*exclusive*) responsibility of the branch manager. Only he or she can take into account factors not amenable to credit scoring such as the personality or the local reputation of the borrower. To come back to your project, I'd like to hear how you can expect to double your **turnover** in one year after having implemented the changes described in your business plan and for which you are requesting a loan.

Jonathan Kervill :
– As explained in our document, my business associate and I train a client's puppy during three consecutive days and nights on our **premises**, after which we return it to its **owner**, who then takes over. In the comfort option, there is a four-day follow-up after the three-day-and-night session: we visit the client late at night and early in the morning at agreed-upon fixed times and take the puppy out to do its business, with a nightly interval short enough to reduce the chance that it will **mess up** (*dirty*) its owner's home. Some puppies need up to four sessions to become fully house-trained and others learn very

quickly. Our approach is professional, it works, we are recommended by several vets (***veterinary surgeons***) and **pet** shops, but a majority of our new clients are referred to us by satisfied customers. Our business grows through word of mouth. We've reached a point where we'll have to refuse new clients if we don't rapidly expand our capacity. Furthermore, some vets have confided to me (*shared with me in confidence*) the average number of puppies they vaccinate each year, from which I infer (*deduce*) that we train only a tiny (*very small*) percentage of our area's puppies, so there is plenty of room for expansion.

Judith Bakerwolt :
– Any competitors yet?

Jonathan Kervill :
– Not to my knowledge, but that wouldn't be a bad thing. It would prove that it's possible to enjoy the company of a dog without the **hassles** and indignities of the first several weeks or months.

Judith Bakerwolt :
– Unless maybe they compete on price?

Jonathan Kervill :
– You've seen our tariffs. They reflect our costs plus a fair margin justified by our know-how (*expertise*), by **exacting** (*very demanding*) working hours and by the value of our services as perceived by customers. I think people would baulk at having their pets trained **on the cheap**. They'd prefer to do it themselves. Apropos of competition, there is more of it in your business than in mine. Did your initial remark about creditworthiness mean I should look somewhere else (*elsewhere*) for my loan?

Judith Bakerwolt :
– Certainly not. I mentioned the point because we always do. We think our clients have a right to know how we handle loan applications. But in the case of a very young entrepreneur like yourself, inquiries rarely produce significant results. And in fact, your loan application has come back from our

headquarters with the observation 'no comments', which allows me to offer you a loan **tailored** to your needs, based on the information you've provided.

Jonathan Kervill :
– And what will that be?

Judith Bakerwolt :
– I propose a five-year unsecured loan of £11,000 at a 9.9% APR (*annualised percentage rate*). It means a monthly payment of £233.23. The total amount to be **repaid** is £13,993.80.

Jonathan Kervill :
– 9.9% seems a very high interest rate! I have a friend whose mortgage is not even half that.

Judith Bakerwolt :
– Yes, that is not at all surprising. A **mortgage loan** is a secured loan, giving the lender the possibility to **repossess** the property to recover the amount loaned, should the borrower **default** (*in case the borrower defaults*). And your friend's mortgage is certainly for a fixed-rate loan. With variable-rate mortgage loans, going rates are as low a 2.8%, but are liable to **shoot up** (*rise suddenly*) later. You could hardly find more favourable terms than 9.9% for an unsecured fixed-rate loan. You qualify for one because you've been a Hollyhock customer for over two years, you have paid each month at least £1,200 into your account, and you have a clean credit record. In the absence of any one of these three conditions, I might still offer you a loan, but the rate would be about double.

Jonathan Kervill :
– OK. Then there is no point in shopping around for a loan.

Judith Bakerwolt :
– I don't think so. These are the papers representing our proposal. Take your time to look at them, and once you've made up your mind, give us a ring (*phone us*). If you wish to go ahead, the contract can be

signed immediately, and the money will be available in your account the next day.

Différents types de compte

There are several types of bank accounts for different purposes, which may be to handle day-to-day transactions, to set money aside for a future use, or to obtain the highest possible interest from one's money.

Comptes courants

The most usual sort of bank account is a transactional account, called current account in the UK and checking account in the USA. As its generic name suggests, it is used to facilitate diverse operations involving money: depositing money into the account, **issuing** or cashing cheques, using a debit card to **withdraw** cash or pay for purchases, arranging **standing orders**, **direct debits** or **giro transfers**.

Autres types de comptes

A **savings account** also allows its holder to make deposits and **withdrawals**, but is much less flexible than a current account. A main difference is that holders of such accounts may not write cheques or use a debit card. Another frequent restriction is a limit to the number of deposits or withdrawals in a given period.

Accounts with a purpose comparable to that of savings accounts are **money market deposit accounts** and **certificates of deposit**. They usually provide higher interest rates than savings accounts.

La banque par Internet

Whenever someone purchases (*buys*) an item (*article*) on the Internet, some kind of Internet banking transaction is involved, usually a payment using a bank card. Internet shopping is thus a dual operation, one facet of which is a commercial transaction between a seller and a buyer who agree about a price and delivery terms, while the other is the payment, a banking operation performed via the Internet.

Beyond their role in Internet shopping, most banks offer their customers various services over the Internet, including the option of accessing accounts. Customers can not only monitor their accounts in real time, i.e. view how they have been affected by the latest transactions, but also initiate operations that do not require a movement of paper, essentially transfer money from their account to another, which may be in the same bank or in another and held by themselves or by another person.

Banks have a long experience regarding the privacy and security of information stored on their computers, and attacks at this level have virtually no chance of succeeding. But there are two weak links in the security chain: the bank customer, and his or her computer. A computer used to access bank accounts should be kept well protected against viruses and potential intruders, particularly if it contains information about bank accounts. The customer may also be targeted directly through **phishing**. This fraud consists in presenting users with a Web page purporting to be their bank's site, and asking them to enter information about their accounts. The victim is taken to the **fake** bank site through a link in an e-mail or sms message supposedly sent by the bank, for example:

"Dear client,
Some of your account details may have been altered as a result of a technical incident. Please use the following link to verify them and correct them if needed."

On the page opened by the link, the dear client is asked to enter his or her account number and secret code. Not being addressed by his or her name immediately raises the suspicion of a normal person, but sent to a million 'dear clients', the **bogus** (*fallacious, fictitious*) message is likely to find a few **compliant** (*acquiescent*) recipients whose accounts can then be **plundered**.

Commentaires

Prononcez correctement !

...you're applying for (*requesting*) a loan – *loan*: this word rimes with *alone, scone, **prone**, **moan*** and should not be confused with ***lawn***, which rimes with ***yawn, prawn, dawn***.

...I like the way you've converted a widespread yet unmet need – *need* is a homophone of the verb ***knead***, and of *kneed* (past of verb *knee = hit with one's knee*). A *k* preceding n is not pronounced. Other examples: *know, **knack**, **knickers**, knife, knight, knob, knock*.

...we are recommended by several vets – *recommend*: words ending with *end* are stressed on the last syllable, e.g. *apprehend, comprehend, intend, descend, condescend, pretend*.

...I think people would baulk at having their pets trained on the cheap – *baulk*: the *l* is not pronounced. Same long vowel sound as in *talk, walk, the Falklands*. Placed between *e* or *i* and *k*, the *l* is pronounced: *milk, **elk***. *Cheap*: long vowel sound, not to be confused with the short *i* in *chip*.

...but are liable to shoot up – *shoot*: the *oo* in *shoot* is a long vowel sound as in *rule, **mood**, rude, root, truce*, not a short one as in *put, cook, took, foot*.

...issuing or cashing cheques – *cheque*: pronounced like *check*, its American version.

...a limit to the number of deposits or withdrawals – *withdrawal*: this word seems to us to have three syllables, but it only has two. The second and last part of the word is pronounced like the French word *drôle*. Another example where we see several syllables where there is only one: the famous *Worcestershire sauce*, in which the combination *orce* is pronounced like the short sound of *oo* in *wood*, or of *u* in *put*.

...a Web page purporting to be their bank's site – *site* is a homophone of ***sight***.

Un homme averti en vaut deux !

...So Mr Kervill – *Mr*, like other abbreviations for a title preceding a family name (*Prof, Dr, Mrs, Ms*) is spelt *Mr.* in American English (also *Mr., Prof., Dr., Mrs., Ms.*).

...I've also read Puppy Housebreaking Ltd's business plan – *Ltd*, abbreviation for *Limited* is written in British English without a full stop at the end.

...with its stuffy old-boy network – *old-boy*, in the phrase *old-boy network*, has nothing to do with our expression *vieux garçon*. It refers to males with some sort of common background (same school or milieu) who use their positions of influence to help one another and sometimes exclude others.

...cigar-smoking smart alecks (*know-it-alls, wise guys, smart asses*) – *smart aleck*: the phrase (*expression*) has no French equivalent, but its three English equivalents can help us **guess** what it means.

...we are as meticulous as any other bank, even more so, actually – *actually* means *in reality, in fact*. It never has the meaning of French *actuellement*, in English *at this time, at present* or *presently*. The French *actualité* is *current events* in English.

...rejecting an application is always the sole (*exclusive*) responsibility – *application* may mean the same as its French homologue, but its most current meaning is *request*, as here.

...a four-day follow-up after the three-day-and-night session: *four-day, three-day-and-night*: the hyphens are used to build compound adjectives. Note that although these adjectives refer to more than one day and more than one night, day and night are spelt without s at the end. The reason: adjectives are invariable in English.

...we are recommended by several vets – *recommend* belongs to a series of words that are spelt with *e* in English and *a* in French: *recommend, correspondence, consistence or consistency, dependent, dependence, independence, current, persistent, persistence.*

...a five-year unsecured loan of £11,000 at a 9.9% APR – *£11,000*: the pound currency symbol £ is placed immediately before the number, and groups of three digits are separated by a comma; 9.9% : English uses a decimal point instead of a decimal comma, and the percent symbol is placed immediately after the number (a space is **mandatory** in French).

...should the borrower default – *default*: this word differs in two ways from the French *défaut.* 1) It is used also as a verb; 2) its meaning as a noun does not include that of *imperfection.*

...and you have a clean credit record – *record* in this context refers to *recorded* (registered) *information*, not to an exceptional performance or circumstance, like the French noun *record.*

...once you have made up your mind, give us a ring – *ring* means here a phone call. *Ring* only has this meaning in British English.

...obtain the highest possible interest from one's money – *interest* is singular. Les intérêts, in this context, are *the interest payments.*

...A savings account – *savings*: in compound words such as *savings bank, savings and loans, savings account, savings* is always plural. As it corresponds to the singular French noun *épargne*, in *caisse d'épargne, compte d'épargne*, we might be tempted to omit the *s* at the end of *savings*.

Des mots qui vont très bien ensemble

...a widespread yet unmet need : *an unmet need, a crying need.*

...one of my preferred flowers : *a preferred flower, a preferred perfume, the solution preferred by the client.*

...the sole (*exclusive*) responsibility of the branch manager : *the branch manager, the country manager, the regional manager, the account manager* (a salesperson in charge of a large customer).

...Not to my knowledge : *to my knowledge, the knowledge society, knowledge workers.*

...They reflect our costs plus a fair margin : *a fair margin, fair trade, a fair share.*

...I mentioned the point because we always do : *to mention a point, to make a point* (to put forward an argument), *you have a point* (this argument of yours is valid), *there is no point in* (it is useless to), *what is the point of* (what is to be gained in), *up to a point, to be on the point of.*

...you have a clean credit record : *a clean credit record, a clean bill of health, to start something with a clean slate.*

...if you wish to go ahead : *to go ahead* (to proceed with something), *to stay ahead, to be ahead of one's time.*

...Direct debits are typically used to settle invoices : *to settle an invoice, to settle a dispute, to settle out of court* (to resolve a dispute through an agreement instead of a suit).

...Internet shopping is thus a dual operation : *a dual operation, a dual situation, a dual role.*

...The victim is taken to the fake bank site : *a fake bank site, a fake doctor, a fake masterpiece, a fake scientific discovery.*

TRUC Des passerelles

...your income has grown steadily (*regularly*) – *regular, regularly*: same meanings as *régulier, régulièrement.*

...let me compliment your bank – *compliment* n v: same meanings as French *compliment, complimenter.*

...a refreshing change from the traditional banking business – *tradition, traditional, traditionally*: same meanings as corresponding French words.

...granting a loan or rejecting an application is always the sole (*exclusive*) responsibility of the branch manager – *response, responsible, responsibility*: same meanings as *réponse, responsable, responsabilité.* But *responsive* (who reacts rapidly) has a different meaning than French *responsif* (relatif à une réponse).

...the personality or the local reputation of the borrower – *reputation, reputed*: same meanings as French *réputation, réputé*. In addition, there is in English the noun *repute* whose meaning is very close to that or *reputation.*

...my business associate and I train a client's puppy during three consecutive days and nights – *associate, associative, association*: same meanings as the corresponding French words. *Consecutive*: same meaning as *consécutif* in French.

...we visit a client late at night – *client, clientele*: same meanings as French *client, clientèle.*

...the number of puppies they vaccinate each year – *vaccine, vaccinate, vaccination*: same meanings as *vaccin, vacciner, vaccination.*

...It would prove that it's possible to enjoy the company of a dog – *possible, impossible, possibility, impossibility*: same meanings as the matching French words.

...You've seen our tariffs – *tariff* n v, same meanings as *tarif, tarifier.* There is no English word resembling French *tarification.*

...your loan application has come back from our headquarters with the observation 'no comment' – *observe, observer, observation, observatory*: same meanings as French *observer, observateur, observation, observatoire.* In addition to the religious meaning of *observant* in French, *observant* in English means 'quick to notice anything'.

...And your friend's mortgage is certainly for a fixed-rate loan – *certain, certainly, certitude*: same meanings as *certain, certainement, certitude.* In addition, English has derived from *certain* the verb *ascertain* (make sure of): you should ascertain the veracity of this statement.

...In the absence of any one of these three conditions – *condition* n v, *conditional, unconditional*: same meanings as *condition, conditionner, conditionnel, inconditionnel.*

...it is used to facilitate diverse operations – *operation, operational, operator*: same meanings as French matching words.

...a main difference is that holders of such accounts – *difference, differential a n, differentiate, differentiation, indifferent, differently, indifferently*: same meanings as the French matching words. The French noun *differend* (désaccord) is rendered in English by the noun *difference.* The English verb *differ* (be different, disagree) cannot be used in the sense *postpone* of the French verb *différer* : *différer un rendez-vous = to postpone an appointment.*

...the other is the payment – *pay* n v, *payer, payment, unpaid* a: mean the same as *paie, payer, payeur* ou *payeuse, paiement, impayé* a. *Un impayé* is *an unpaid bill* in English.

...including the option of accessing accounts – *opt, option, optional* mean the same as *opter, option, optionnel* in French.

...may have been altered as a result of a technical incident – *result* n v: same meanings as *résultat, résulter.*

...use the following link to verify them – *verify, verification*: same meanings as *vérifier, vérification.*

...Not being addressed by his or her name immediately raises the suspicion – *suspect* a n v, *suspicion, suspicious*: same meanings as *suspect, suspecter, suspicion, suspicieux* in French. In addition, *suspicious* also means *qui éveille des soupçons.*

Vocabulaire anglais/français

appoint	nommer
bogus	bidon
certificate of deposit	certificat de dépôt
compliant	d'accord, consentant
congratulate	féliciter
dawn	aube
default	non paiement, s'abstenir de payer
direct debit	prélèvement bancaire
elk	renne
exacting	très pénible (horaire, travail)
fake	factice
giro transfer	virement bancaire
gather	comprendre, inférer

guess	deviner
hassle	tracas
hollyhock	rose trémière
housebreak	éduquer (un animal) à la propreté
housetraining	dressage à la propreté
issue	émettre
knack	aptitude, talent
knead	pétrir
knickers (Brit)	slip de femme
lawn	gazon
loan	emprunt
lure	attirer, leurrer
mandatory	obligatoire
mess up	salir
moan	gémir
money market deposit account	compte monétaire
mood	humeur
mortgage loan	prêt hypothécaire
on the cheap	au rabais
owner	propriétaire
pet	animal de compagnie
phishing	hameçonnage
plunder	dévaliser
prawn	grosse crevette
premises	locaux (d'une entreprise)
prone	ayant tendance à
puppy	chiot
rating agency	agence de notation

repay	rembourser
repossess	prendre possession de (faute de paiement)
savings account	compte d'épargne
shoot up	augmenter brusquement
standing order	ordre de virement permanent
stuffy	étouffant
tailor	tailler (sur mesure)
turnover	chiffre d'affaires
unmet	non satisfait (besoin)
veterinary surgeon	vétérinaire
withdraw	retirer
withdrawal	retrait
yawn	bailler

Annexe

Deux bouées de sauvetage

L'élaboration d'une phrase est un processus inconscient. Notre subconscient sélectionne chaque mot dans des ensembles de formes ayant un point commun mais présentant des différences : formes d'un verbe variables selon la personne ou le temps, substantif, verbe, adjectif ou adverbe de même racine, mots exprimant diverses nuances d'une même idée, mots de sonorités voisines mais distincts par le sens, mots de même sens dans des langues différentes.

Ces différences déterminent le choix d'un mot d'un ensemble et lui permettent d'apporter du sens à la phrase : présent plutôt que futur ou passé ; singulier et non pluriel ; ce mot-ci avec un son de voyelle long et non celui-là avec un son de voyelle court. Les associations possibles n'étant pas limitées, un même terme peut théoriquement appartenir à une infinité d'ensembles différents. Plus un mot a d'associations diverses avec d'autres mots, plus il a de chances de trouver place dans la phrase en construction.

Pour mettre en œuvre ce mécanisme, notre subconscient doit disposer de nombreux ensembles de mots. C'est la pratique d'une langue qui les constitue peu à peu, à mesure que nous remarquons ces différences qui apportent du sens. Nous les remarquons d'autant plus vite qu'elles sont plus marquées. Et nous mettons très longtemps à prendre conscience de certaines différences, notamment entre l'anglais et le français, parce qu'elles n'empêchent pas de comprendre.

Si notre vocabulaire est lacunaire et si chacun de ses éléments n'est pas relié à d'autres par des associations suffisamment nombreuses, nous avons du mal à nous exprimer.

Les textes de cet ouvrage ont étoffé votre vocabulaire anglais, et ses commentaires vous ont aidé à bâtir ces associations multiples nécessaires à l'expression spontanée. Ils ont aussi attiré votre attention sur des différences entre le français et l'anglais que vous risquiez de ne jamais remarquer. Le livre ne vous a pas rendu bilingue français/anglais, mais il vous a permis de faire une partie du chemin. Voyant qu'il ne vous a coûté que quelques euros, un écossais dirait *It's good value for your money.*

Vous trouverez désormais plus souvent l'expression anglaise adaptée lors de la rédaction d'un texte anglais, surtout dans le cadre professionnel. Mais l'anglais dont vous avez besoin ne vous viendra pas toujours à l'esprit. À la place, votre subconscient vous proposera des mots français dont vous ne savez que faire. Comme dit cette image anglaise traduisant l'embarras, *you are at sea*. Raccrochez-vous alors à l'une des deux bouées de sauvetage de l'annexe, en anglais *life buoys*.

La première, intitulée Passerelles, reprend dans l'ordre alphabétique tous les mots anglais identiques à des mots français ou de forme voisine et ayant les mêmes sens, cités dans les commentaires. Si vous y trouvez des mots ressemblant à ceux que vous propose votre subconscient, utilisez-les !

La seconde, Vocabulaire français/anglais, liste dans l'ordre alphabétique tous les termes français des lexiques anglais/français de fin de chapitre. En regard de chaque terme français figure un ou plusieurs mots anglais avec l'indication du numéro du chapitre où ils apparaissent. Si un mot anglais vous paraît convenir, utilisez-le. En cas de doute, reportez-vous à son chapitre (où il figure en gras) pour vérifier par le biais du contexte d'utilisation s'il correspond à ce que vous voulez dire.

TRUC Passerelles

Attention ! Les mots sont parfois suivis d'abréviations pour vous aider à savoir s'il s'agit d'un verbe (v), d'un adjectif (a) ou d'un nom (n), d'un mot au pluriel (pl).

A

abound, abundance, abundant, abundantly; act (n v), action, activity, actor; adhere (v), adherence, adherent (a n), adhesion; adjacent; aide-mémoire; analysis; antithesis; associate, association, associative; attention, attentionate; automatic, automatically, automaton (pl automata); autonomous, autonomously, autonomy

B

basis; biological; bon mot; carte blanche

C

central, centralisation, centralise, centrally, centre (n v); certain, certainly, certitude, clarification; clarify, clarity, clear; client, clientele; comme ci, comme ça; comme il faut; comparable, comparative, comparatively, comparator, compare, comparison; condition (n v), conditional; contribute, contribution, contributor; conversation, conversational, converse v; correspond, correspondence, correspondent; coup d'état; coup de grace; crisis; cycle; de rigueur;

D

decentralisation, decentralise; dense, density; depend, dependence, dependent; difference, differential (a n), differentiate, differentiation, differently; disciple, disciplinary, discipline; displace, displacement;

E

egocentric; emigrant, emigrate, emigration; éminence grise; emphasis; entre nous; exist, existence, existent, existential; expert, expertise

F

fait accompli; familiar, familiarisation, familiarise, familiarity, family; faux pas; femme fatale

G

gradual, gradually

H

hypothesis, hypothetical, hypothetically

I

ill at ease, ill humour, ill-assorted, ill-conceived, ill-defined, ill-disposed, ill-gotten, ill-humoured, ill-treat, ill-treatment; immigrant, immigrate, immigration; impossibility , impossible; incomparable; independence, independent, independently; indicate, indication, indicator; indifferent, indifferently; inform (v), informant (n); ingredient; innovate, innovation, innovative, innovator; introduce, introduction, introductory; invent (v), invention, inventor; invest, investiture, investment, investor

M

maître d'hôtel; majority; metal, metallic, metallisation, metallise; migrate, migration; mot juste

N

necessary, necessitate, necessity

O

observant (a), observation, observatory, observe, observer (n); obtain, obtainable, obtention; operation, operational, operator; opt, option, optional

P

pay (n v), payer (n), payment; place, placement; placid, placidity, placidly; position; possibility, possible; present (a n v), presentable, presentation, presenter (n); profess (v), profession, profession of faith, professional, professionalism, professor; profit (n v), profitability, profitable, profitably

R

raison d'être; recycle (v), recycling; reduce, reducible, reduction; regular, regularly; replace, replacement;

represent; reputation, reputed; response, responsibility, responsible; result (n v); revolution, revolutionary, revolutionise

S

savoir faire; sign (v n), signatory (n), signature, significant, signification, signify; similar, similarly; special, specialisation, specialise, specialist; suspect (a n v), suspicion, suspicious; synthesis, synthesise, synthetic

T

table, tablet; tariff (n v); technical, technically, technician; thesis; tradition, traditional, traditionally; transport (n), transport (v);

U

unconditional; unpaid (a)

V

vaccinate (v), vaccination, vaccine (n); verification, verify.

Vocabulaire français/anglais

Français	*Anglais (+ chapitre)*
à la pointe du progrès	**state-of-the-art 3**
à l'intérieur de	**within 3**
à ma connaissance	**to my knowledge 3**
à plat	**flat 3**
à toute épreuve	**foolproof 9**
à trois volets (litt. à trois dents de fourche)	**three-pronged 5**
à venir	**forthcoming 1**
aborder (un sujet)	**broach 3**
abrupt	**steep 4**
accélérer	**speed up 6**

accorder une moindre importance à	**deemphasize 1**
accueillir	**entertain 6**
achèvement	**completion 3**
achever	**complete 3**
actif	**assets 7**
actifs circulants	**current assets 7**
actionnaire	**shareholder 1, 3**
actionnaire	**stockholder 1, 7**
actions	**stocks 7**
adoucir	**soften 3**
affuter	**hone 2**
agence de notation	**credit rating agency 11**
agent immobilier (brit.)	**real-estate agent 7**
agent immobilier (am.)	**realtor 7**
agile	**nimble 9**
aider (à malfaire)	**abet 10**
aiguillage, aiguiller	**switch n v 2**
alcool (familier)	**booze 5**
aller en bateau	**sail v 8**
aller et venir	**ply 2**
animal de compagnie	**pet 11**
annonce	**ad (advertisement) 1**
annoncer	**herald 2**
appareil électrique	**electrical appliance 10**
appartement	**flat (Brit.) 10**
appartenir	**belong 3**
appel local	**local call 5**
appelant	**caller 5**
approprié	**relevant 5**

aptitude	**knack 11**
arbitre	**referee 3**
argumentaire de vente	**sales pitch 8**
arrangement	**setup 2**
arrêt	**standstill 2**
arrivée	**advent 10**
arriver à	**reach 1**
arriver à maturité	**come of age 2**
article (d'un contrat)	**provision 3**
assurance	**insurance 4**
atteindre	**reach 1, 8**
attirer	**lure 11**
au milieu de	**amidst 1**
au rabais	**on the cheap 11**
augmentation (de salaire)	**raise (Am.), rise (Brit.) 9**
augmenter brusquement	**shoot up 11**
authentique	**genuine 1**
automate bancaire	**cash dispenser 5**
automatique	**knee-jerk 3**
autopartage	**car sharing 2**
autorisé à	**entitled to 9**
autoroute	**motorway (Brit.) 2**
autoroute	**expressway (Am.) 2**
autoroute à péage	**turnpike (Am.) 2**
autre possibilité	**alternative 9**
avantage	**edge 1**
avoir besoin de	**require 3**
avoir en magasin	**carry 10**
avoir mal	**to be in pain 5**

ayant tendance à	**prone to 11**
balance	**scales 10**
balayer	**sweep 2**
banlieue	**suburb 2**
bâtiment	**building 7**
bénéfice brut	**gross profit 7**
bénéfice d'exploitation	**operating income 7**
bien immobilier	**real estate 7**
bilan	**balance sheet 7**
biologique	**organic 2**
bois	**wood 8**
boîte	**can 6**
bonnes dispositions	**goodwill 1**
bouillonner	**gush 2**
bourse de valeurs	**stock exchange 3**
brancher	**plug 5**
but	**goal 5**
cadre	**framework 4, 9**
café au lait	**white coffee 2**
candidat	**applicant 1**
candidature	**application 1**
carnet de commandes	**order book 9**
carrefour	**intersection 5**
carton	**cardboard 7**
centre commercial	**shopping mall 10**
cérémonie	**function 8**
certificat de dépôt	**certificate of deposit 11**
chanceler	**stagger 2**
charge de travail	**workload 3**
chef de service	**department manager 3**

chiffre d'affaires	**turnover 7, 11**
chiffrement	**encryption 3**
chiffrement des données	**data encryption 3**
choquer	**aback (take someone) 1**
chose prononcée	**utterance 5**
cible	**target 6**
client	**customer 7**
client potentiel	**potential customer 1**
colle	**glue 1**
comprendre	**gather 11**
comptabilité	**accounting 3, 7**
comptabilité	**bookkeeping 7**
comptabilité en partie double	**double-entry bookkeeping 7**
compte d'épargne	**savings account 11**
compte d'exploitation	**income statement 7**
compte monétaire	**money market deposit account 11**
compte tenu de	**in view of 6**
compte-rendu de réunion	**minutes 3**
comptes clients	**accounts payable 7**
concerné	**relevant 6**
concerner	**pertain to 5, 6**
confirmer la réception ou compréhension	**acknowledge 5**
confiserie	**sweet shop (Brit.) 10**
confiserie	**candy store (Am.) 10**
confronté à	**confronted with 8**
consacré par l'usage	**time-honoured 8**
consacrer	**devote 8**

consentant	**compliant 11**
considérer	**deem 3**
considérer comme	**deem 6**
constamment	**continuously 8**
contentieux	**litigation 6**
continu	**continuous 8**
continuel	**continual 8**
continuellement	**continually 8**
continuer	**pursue 7, endure 4**
continûment	**continuously 8**
contribuer efficacement à	**to go a long way towards 5**
corbeau	**raven 3**
cordonnier	**cobbler 2**
correspondance, correspondre	**match 5**
cotée (entreprise, société)	**listed 7**
cotisation	**contribution 4**
cotisation	**premium 4**
coup	**blow 9**
courant alternatif	**alternating current 10**
courant continu	**direct current 10**
couverture	**rug 3**
covoiturage	**car-pooling 2**
covoiturage	**car-pooling 6**
création	**inception 1**
crucial, grave	**fateful 3**
d'accord	**compliant 11**
dans son esprit	**in one's mind's eye 5**
dans tout le (toute la)	**throughout 3**

de banlieue	**suburban 10**
de conseil	**advisory 8**
de court (prendre quelqu'un)	**aback (take someone) 1**
de courte durée	**short-lived 6**
de front	**abreast 1**
de grande dimension	**sizeable 3**
de même nature que	**akin to 1**
de toutes sortes	**in all walks of life 2**
de travers	**awry 1**
débarrasser	**rid 1, 10**
débiteur	**debtor 7**
débrancher	**unplug 5**
début	**inception 1**
décennie	**decade 4**
déchaîner	**unleash 2**
décharge	**landfill 6**
déchiqueter	**shred 6**
déchirer	**rip 2**
déchirer	**rip 9**
décider	**settle 9**
décideur	**decision maker 9**
déclencher	**trigger 1, 3**
dédié à	**dedicated to 6**
demande de proposition	**request for proposal (RFP) 3**
demeuré	**moron 5**
dépasser	**overshoot 3**
dépendant de	**dependent (up)on 8**
dépendre de	**depend (up)on 8**

dépenses de personnel	**payroll expenses 7**
dépenses d'exploitation	**operating expenses 7**
déroute	**rout 8**
désagrément	**hassle 10**
désirer fortement	**crave 8**
désormais	**henceforth 10**
destinataire	**addressee 3**
destinataire	**recipient 6**
destiné à	**dedicated to 6**
détenu	**convict 1**
détestable	**obnoxious 8**
détruire complètement	**obliterate 7**
dette	**debt 7**
dette hypothécaire à court terme	**mortgage payment 7**
dette hypothécaire à long terme	**mortgage balance 7**
dévaliser	**plunder 11**
deviner	**guess 11**
devise	**currency 7**
dévorer	**eat up 3**
dilemme	**conundrum 2**
dimension	**size 3**
directeur général	**CEO (chief executive officer) 7**
dirigeant	**executive 7**
discours pour convaincre (commerce, politique)	**pitch 1**
disponible	**available 3**
distraire	**entertain 6**

domaine	**area 3**
douleur intense	**agony 10**
durée de vie	**lifespan 6**
échange	**trade 7**
échapper	**elude 8**
échelle sociale	**social ladder 4**
effectuer	**complete 10**
effet de levier	**leverage 7**
efficacité	**efficacy 8**
effort, s'efforcer	**endeavour n v 5**
élection	**poll 8**
embarras	**quandary 2**
embaucher	**hire 1**
embouteillages	**traffic congestion 2**
émettre	**issue 11**
émeute	**riot 1**
empreinte	**footprint 6**
empressement	**eagerness 1**
emprunt	**loan 7, 11**
en accord (avec)	**consistent (with) 4**
en amont	**upstream 2**
en aval	**downstream 6**
en fait	**actually 6**
en jeu	**at stake 3**
en pente (très)	**steep 4**
en retard	**belated 3**
en vue de	**with a view to 6**
encourager	**foster 2**
engagé	**committed 3**
enjamber	**straddle 2**

enjeu	**stake 2, 8**
ennui	**boredom 4**
enquête	**survey 6**
enquête d'opinion	**poll 8**
enthousiaste	**keen 6**
entier	**integer 7**
entraîner	**incur 3**
entraîner	**entail 3**
épeler	**spell 5**
espèces	**cash 7**
esprit	**wit 2**
esprit	**mind 5**
estimation	**assessment 3**
estimer	**appraise 3**
estimer	**assess 3**
étouffant	**stuffy 11**
évidemment	**obviously 3**
exactitude	**accuracy 1**
exclure	**rule out 1**
expert	**assessor 3**
expert d'assurance	**insurance assessor 3**
exploit	**feat 4**
exposer (dépense)	**incur 7**
exprimer	**utter 3**
extrait	**excerpt 8**
factice	**fake 11**
faillite	**bankruptcy 7**
faire attention à	**mind 5**
faire discrètement allusion à	**hint at 9**

faire face à (une situation, une charge de travail)	**cope with 3**
faire l'éloge de	**extoll 1**
faire la connaissance de	**meet 1**
faire la vaisselle	**wash up 9**
faire l'éloge de	**praise 3**
faire un somme	**snooze 5**
famille	**household 10**
famille (de lions)	**pride 6**
faubourgs	**outskirts 2**
favoriser	**foster 7**
féliciter	**congratulate 11**
feuille de tableur	**spreadsheet 6**
final	**eventual 8, 9**
finalement	**eventually 1**
focalisé	**focused 6**
fondamental	**of the essence 6**
fonds de pension	**pension fund 4**
fonds propres	**owners' equity 7**
fournir	**come up with 10**
fournisseur	**supplier 3, 7**
fournisseur de services Internet	**Internet Service Provider 5**
frais généraux	**selling and general administrative expenses 7**
frappant	**striking 6**
frapper	**hit 9**
frein, freiner	**brake n v 2, 5**
fuir (liquide ou gaz), fuite	**leak v n 9**

GAB (guichet automatique de banque)	**ATM (automatic teller machine) 5**
gains	**earnings 7**
gamme de produits	**product range 8**
Gestion des Ressouves Humaines	**HRM (Human Resources Management) 6**
glisser	**slip 9**
gonfler	**inflate 6**
grade	**rank 4**
grand magasin	**department store 10**
grande misère	**penury 9**
grande société	**corporation 3**
groupe	**pool 3**
guérir	**heal 2**
habiter	**inhabit 2**
hameçonnage	**phishing 11**
hauteur (du ton)	**pitch 1**
hebdomadaire	**weekly 3**
homologue	**opposite number 8**
horaires flexibles	**flexitime 2**
horrifier	**appall 10**
hostilité	**ill will 1**
humeur	**mood 11**
immobilisations	**long-term assets 7**
impliquer	**imply 3**
impôt	**tax 4**
incertain	**moot 3**
incidence	**impact 3**
inciter (à mal faire)	**abet 10**
inciter à	**induce 3**

incommode pour	**awkward for 1**
inconvénient	**downside, drawback 6**
inférer	**gather 11**
inhabitable	**uninhabitable 2**
inondé	**awash 1**
insecte nuisible	**pest 5**
intention	**purpose 3**
introduire	**usher in 10**
inventaire	**inventory 10**
inversement	**conversely 9**
jaillir	**spurt 2**
jauger	**appraise 3**
jeton	**token 7**
laine	**wool 1**
laisser s'écouler	**leak 6**
le premier	**the former 10**
le second	**the latter 10**
lente	**nit 10**
leurrer	**lure 11**
location de voitures	**car hire (Brit.) car rental (Am.) 2**
locaux (d'une entreprise)	**premises 2, 6, 11**
logiciels d'entreprise	**enterprise software 7**
lot (expédié)	**consignment 5**
lourd de conséquences	**momentous 3**
mal nécessaire	**necessary evil 3**
malencontreux	**unfortunate 3**
marché d'actions	**stock market 7**
marge	**margin 7**
marge bénéficiaire	**profit margin 7**

marge brute d'autofinancement	**cash flow 7**
marge de manœuvre	**leeway 2**
méritoire	**commendable, laudable, praiseworthy 6**
métier	**trade 7**
mettre en commun	**pool 3**
mettre en lumière	**highlight 7**
mission	**assignment 3**
mutation	**move 9**
nécessiter	**require 1**
néfaste	**harmful 3**
neurogenèse	**neurogenesis 4**
niveau	**level 3**
niveau de qualité	**grade 4**
nocif	**harmful 6**
nommer	**appoint 11**
non paiement	**default 11**
non satisfait (besoin)	**unmet 11**
nourrir (un animal)	**feed 10**
obligation	**bond 7**
obligatoire	**compulsory 4**
obligatoire	**mandatory 4, 11**
obliger	**compel 5**
obstacle	**hurdle 1**
offre	**bid 1, 2**
ohé	**ahoy 1**
ordonnance	**prescription 5**
ordre de virement permanent	**standing order 11**

ordre du jour (d'une réunion)	**agenda 3**
origine	**inception 1**
par répartition	**pay-as-you-go 4**
par suite	**hence 9**
participer à	**participate in 8**
partie prenante	**stakeholder 3**
passage	**stint 2**
passif	**liabilities 7**
pénurie	**dearth 9**
pépier	**chirp 2**
PER ou quotient C/B (cours/bénéfice par action)	**price/earning ratio 7**
perdre	**lose 5**
personnel	**staff 1**
personnel de bord	**in-flight personnel 8**
perte	**loss 6**
phrase (grammaire)	**sentence 8**
pièce de monnaie	**coin 7**
pièce jointe	**attachment 6**
piéton	**pedestrian 2, 6**
pile	**battery 6, 10**
piller	**plunder 11**
pitoyable	**pathetic 2**
place (de parking)	**slot 6**
plage	**beach 8**
pleurer	**weep 9**
poing	**fist 10**
point de vente	**point of sale 10**
point final	**full stop 7**

poste disponible	**job vacancy 1**
poursuivre	**pursue 7**
pratiquement	**virtually 3**
précédent (adj)	**previous 3**
préjugé	**prejudice 4**
prélèvement bancaire	**direct debit 11**
préliminaire	**tentative 1**
prémisse	**premise 2**
prendre en compte	**accommodate 9**
prendre possession de (faute de paiement)	**repossess 11**
présider	**chair 3**
presse professionnelle	**trade press 1, 7**
prêt hypothécaire	**mortgage loan 11**
prétendre	**purport 1**
prévisible	**foreseeable 3, 6**
prévision	**forecast 3**
prime (d'assurance)	**premium 4**
prison	**gaol (Brit.), jail (Am.) 1**
prisonnier	**gaolbird 1**
prix de revient	**cost of revenue 7**
produire	**produce 2**
produire	**come up with 10**
produit de l'agriculture	**produce 2**
projet en cours	**ongoing project 3**
proposition (grammaire)	**clause 8**
proposition, faire une proposition	**bid n, v 3**
proprement dit(e)	**proper 4**
propriétaire	**owner 11**

provoquer	**entail 3**
qualifications	**credentials 1**
quasi insurmontable	**intractable 2**
querelle	**row 7**
qui à droit à	**eligible 4**
qui ne va pas	**amiss 1**
rangée	**row 7**
râper	**grate 2**
rassembler	**gather 2**
ratio de l'indépendance financière	**equity ratio 7**
ratio de liquidité	**current ratio 7**
ravi	**delighted 3**
réaliser (une vente)	**complete (a sale) 1**
réalité	**actuality 1**
rechercher	**look for 1**
rechercher	**seek 10**
récolte, récolter	**harvest n v 3**
récolter	**reap 2, 4**
récompenser	**reward 6**
reconnaître la présence ou l'importance de	**acknowledge 3**
rédiger	**write down 3**
redoutable	**daunting 1**
réfections	**rework 3**
règle	**rule 9**
régler	**settle 3, 9**
regrouper	**pool 3**
rejoindre	**join 6**
relatif à	**pertaining to 8**

relire	**proofread 1**
rembourser	**repay 11**
rencontrer	**meet with 1**
rendement des capitaux propres	**return on equity 7**
rendre inutile	**obviate 3, 10**
repas	**meal 2**
repère	**landmark 2**
représentant du personnel	**employee representative 6**
respecter (une loi)	**abide by 9**
rester en ligne	**hold on 5**
résultat	**outcome 8**
résulter	**accrue 3**
retard	**delay 3**
retirer	**withdraw 11**
retrait	**withdrawal 11**
retraite	**retirement 4**
réunion	**meeting 3**
réunion de direction	**board meeting 3**
réussir à obtenir	**secure 9**
rotation du stock	**inventory turnover 7**
rouleau	**roll 8**
s'abstenir de payer	**default 11**
salutation	**greeting 5**
sans faille	**foolproof 9**
s'avérer	**prove 9**
savoir faire	**skill 9**
se lancer dans	**take up 4**
se maintenir	**endure 4**

se pencher	**stoop 3**
se pencher sur	**pore 10**
se produire	**occur 9**
se rendre au travail et en revenir	**commute v 2**
s'effondrer	**break down, collapse 4**
selon	**depending on 3**
s'engager à	**commit to 3**
sensible	**sensitive 6**
sévère	**stiff 3**
siège	**head office 3**
signal	**cue 2**
signe annonciateur	**bellwether, harbinger 2**
significatif	**meaningful 6**
s'incliner devant	**bow to 9**
s'infilter (liquide)	**seep 9**
situation matrimoniale	**marital status 1**
société cotée	**public company 1, 7**
société de distribution	**retail company 7**
solide	**sturdy 10**
somme	**snooze n 5**
sonnerie	**ring 5**
sorte	**kind 3**
souci	**concern 3**
soulèvement	**upheaval 1**
soulever (une question)	**bring up 3**
souligner	**underscore 1**
stade	**stage 1, 5**
stage	**internship 2**
stagiaire	**intern 2**

stock	**inventory 7, 10**
stratégies d'ensemble	**overall strategies 3**
strict	**stringent 6**
subordonné à	**subject to 8**
suite de quelques mots	**phrase 8**
suivant	**following 3**
sujet à discussion	**moot 3**
supposition	**assumption 4**
surabondance	**glut 9**
surgir	**crop up 3**
surmonter	**contend with 2**
survaleur	**goodwill 1**
surveiller	**monitor 3**
susciter	**breed 5**
syndicat	**trade union 7, 9**
système PRT	**Personal Rapid Transit 2**
tableau papier	**flip chart 7**
tailler (sur mesure)	**tailor 11**
talent	**skill 9, knack 11**
tas	**heap 4**
technologie de l'information	**IT (Information Technology) 3**
téléphoner à	**ring (Brit.) 5**
tenir (quelqu'un) au courant	**keep (someone) abreast 3**
tenir au courant (se)	**keep abreast 3**
tenter sa chance	**try one's luck 10**
test de réception	**acceptance test 3**
tirer	**pull 3**
tirer brusquement	**tug 3**

titres	**securities 4**
titre négociable	**marketable security 7**
tordre, ajuster	**tweak 1**
tour (échecs)	**rook 3**
tourbe	**peat 4**
tourner	**revolve 2**
tracas	**hassle 11**
traiter	**handle 3**
traiter	**address 6**
trajet	**commute n 2**
trancher	**slit 1**
transports en commun	**mass transit 2**
travail à distance	**telecommuting, telework 2**
travailler dur	**toil 2**
très pénible (horaire, travail)	**exacting 11**
trier	**sort out 6**
trophée	**trophy 4**
troupeau	**herd 6**
ultérieur	**further 6**
usine	**plant 6**
valeur comptable	**book value 7**
venue	**advent 10**
versements au titre de la retraite	**retirement benefits 4**
verser	**pour 10**
veuve	**widow 5**
virement bancaire	**giro transfer 11**
vitesse	**speed 5**

vœu, faire le vœu de	**vow 7, 9**
vol	**theft 3**

Disponibles dans la collection « Pour les Nuls »

Langues

Guides de conversation

Titre	*Auteur*	*Prix*	*ISBN*
Le Basque	Charles Videgain	5,90 €	978-2-7540-1239-3
Le Breton	Hervé Le Bihan	5,90 €	978-2-7540-1240-9
Le Japonais	Eriko Sato, Vincent Grépinet	5,90 €	978-2-7540-0653-8
L'Arabe	Amine Bouchentouf, Sylvie Chraïbi, Aboubakr Chraïbi	5,90 €	978-2-7540-0839-6
Le Portugais	Karen Keller, Ricardo Rodrigues	5,90 €	978-2-7540-1016-0
Le Russe	Vincent Bénet, Oleg Chinkarouk, Serafima Gettys, Andrew Kaufman	5,90 €	978-2-7540-1010-8
L'Allemand	Paulina Christensen, Claude Raimond	5,90 €	978-2-7540-0324-7
L'Italien	Francesca Onofri, Sylvie Le Bras	5,90 €	978-2-7540-0325-4
Le Chinois	Wendy Abraham, Joël Bellassen	5,90 €	978-2-7540-0485-5
Le Néerlandais	Margreet Kwakernaak, Michael Hofland, Annick Christiaens	5,90 €	978-2-7540-0484-8
L'Espagnol	Suzanna Wald, Anne-Carole Grillot	5,90 €	978-2-7540-0178-6
L'Anglais	Gail Brenner, Claude Raimond	5,90 €	978-2-7540-0177-9

Kits audio

Titre	*Auteur*	*Prix*	*ISBN*
Kit audio Anglais	Gail Brenner	17,90 €	978-2-7540-0963-8
Kit audio Espagnol	Jessica Langemeier	17,90 €	978-2-7540-0964-5
Kit audio italien	Tereza L. Picarazzi et Sylvie Le Bras	17,90 €	978-2-7540-1328-4
Kit audio chinois	Mengjun Liu et Mike Packerics	17,90 €	978-2-7540-1329-1

… en Poche

Titre	*Auteur*	*Prix*	*ISBN*
L'Anglais correct	Claude Raimond	11,90 €	978-2-8769-1923-5